ABINGDON & WITNEY COLLEGE

R41872 0805

Library and Resour
Abingdon Campus

D0588429

AB

8092

abingdon&witney college
Wootton Road
Abingdon OX14 1GG
01235 216240

Also by James Clarke

The Pocket Essentials: George Lucas
The Virgin Film Guide: Coppola

Steven Spielberg

James Clarke

www.pocketessentials.com

This second edition, first published in Great Britain 2004 by Pocket Essentials,
P.O. Box 394, Harpenden, Herts, AL5 1JX

Distributed in the USA by Trafalgar Square Publishing, PO Box 257, Howe Hill
Road, North Pomfret, Vermont 05053

http://www.noexit.co.uk

Copyright © James Clarke 2004

The right of James Clarke to be identified as the author of this work has been
asserted by him in accordance with the Copyright, Designs and Patents Act 1988.

All rights reserved. No part of this book may be reproduced, stored in or introduced
into a retrieval system, or transmitted, in any form, or by any means (electronic,
mechanical, photocopying, recording or otherwise) without the written permission
of the publisher. Any person who does any unauthorised act in relation to this
publication may be liable to criminal prosecution and civil claims for damages. The
book is sold subject to the condition that it shall not, by way of trade or otherwise,
be lent, re-sold, hired out or otherwise circulated, without the publisher's prior
consent, in any form or binding or cover other than in which it is published, and
without similar conditions, including this condition being imposed on the subsequent
publication.

A CIP catalogue record for this book is available from the British Library.

ISBN 1 904048 29 3

9 8 7 6 5 4 3 2 1

Book typeset by Avocet Typeset, Chilton, Aylesbury, Bucks
Printed and bound by in Great Britain by Cox & Wyman, Reading, Berks

For Mum and Dad and Leela Kapeela

Contents

CONTENTS

Introduction

'There's a rescue mission involved in the best movies. And that person is saved from his own undoing or what other people are doing to him. You have to bring people down to the bottom before you can recover in an operatic third finale.'

Steven Spielberg, Rolling Stone, 1985

As the summer of 2001 cooled, Steven Spielberg's latest movie *AI: Artificial Intelligence* divided, confounded and frustrated critics and audiences who had been expecting something akin to the 'warm embrace' (to quote Spielberg) of *Close Encounters of the Third Kind* and *ET: The Extra Terrestrial*. Instead, the new movie fused the chilling, the unsettling, the breathtaking and the melancholy. It wasn't as easy on the heart and mind as his other fantasy pieces had been. The film did not leave audiences with an up feeling but instead a real sense of sadness as David, the boy robot at the heart of the story, seeks out his place in the world and the approval that comes with love.

Staying true to the apparently exhausting but, for audiences, hugely welcome multi-picture pace that he established in 1989, Spielberg followed *AI* with *Minority Report* (far more Kubrick inflected than *AI* ironically) and then

9

the lighter, brighter but still emotionally resonant caper chase movie *Catch Me If You Can*. Without doubt, Spielberg's ever strengthening interest in diversity (at least on the surface) in his choice of screenplays was apparent to all. At the time of *Minority Report's* release Spielberg noted 'Not a lot of scepticism has gotten into my work ... I feel as I've gotten older, I've gotten more courageous.' (WIRED, June 2003, *Spielberg in The Twilight Zone*, by Lisa Kennedy, pp. 106–113, p. 146 – this excerpt from p. 112)

By 2003, Spielberg's TV producing track record had also proved compelling evidence of his contribution to small screen pop culture, on a wide-ranging scale. In autumn 2001, American TV broadcast the mini series *Band of Brothers*, which followed American citizen soldiers under fire in Europe during World War Two. Based on the book of the same name by historian, the late Stephen J. Ambrose, and something of an expansion of the milieu of Spielberg's 1998 hit *Saving Private Ryan*, *Band of Brothers* was a hugely successful project, which looks to be succeeded soon enough by another Spielberg supervised World War II series set in the Pacific Theatre of War.

In contrast to the historical realism of *Band of Brothers* (its opening credits sequence and theme music by Michael Kamen were exquisite), Spielberg was also the executive producer of *Taken*, a science fiction series that spanned the second half of the twentieth century, dramatising encounters with extra terrestrial life. The opening episode, directed by Tobe Hooper who had achieved great things twenty years before with the film *Poltergeist* (incidentally based on a Spielberg storyline), recalled *Close Encounters of the Third Kind* and Spielberg's *Amazing Stories* episode *The Mission (1985)*. The series was a massive hit, reminding us of the allure of the 'great out there' and Spielberg's take on it. Film critic J. Hoberman wasn't far off the mark when commenting that: 'If there is a universal personality in contemporary cinema it is surely Steven Spielberg.'(Sight and Sound, p. 16, Sept 2001, *The Dreamlife of Androids*)

In 2002, Spielberg's film *ET: The Extra Terrestrial* was released in a Special Edition format which saw several amendments to shots (for example ET is shown running as a full figure in their attempt to catch a ride home and later in the film ET is shown submerged beneath the water in a bath). The amendments certainly did not detract or radically alter the tone of the film at all. Only the digital removal of rifles from the police, as they try to stop the boys on their bikes in the film's big chase sequence, took away some of the impending peril of the moment.

What was most surprising, however, was the muted response to the re-release, given the huge success of George Lucas's *Star Wars* Special Edition releases of 1997. Whatever the changes, *ET: The Extra Terrestrial* in its twentieth anniversary incarnation remained as affecting as ever and yet audiences did not turn out in the numbers perhaps expected. Was the film just too gentle for the moviegoers of 2002 who had become accustomed to ever faster paced and abrasive fantasy movies? Was it just that people had seen it too many times on TV and video by then to feel a theatrical visit was warranted? Ultimately, the *ET* re-release reminded those who saw it of just how gentle the film is and how accomplished Spielberg's balance of the fanciful, comic and tender was. It also stands in enough contrast to Spielberg's later, less sunny and more obviously upbeat movies.

The unease and sense of a morally uncertain world that had been so central to *Schindler's List,* the watershed movie of Spielberg's mid-career, has continued to enrich the director's films made since 1993 and has demonstrated just how compelling Hollywood cinema can be when it uses genre to explore ethical dilemmas. The Steven Spielberg of today is a different filmmaker than the one who came to the fore in the late 1970s and early 1980s and this evolution is constantly intriguing.

Seeing Through Spielberg's Eyes

It has often been noted that a translation of the name Spielberg brings us to what is almost too neat a meaning: play mountain. It is a suitable tag for a storyteller whose films have so often converted life into a playground, in which characters learn and are illuminated about their own potential. His films as a whole, as an experience, could be said to work in this way, and on many occasions this sense of playfulness is spiked with a very vivid sense of menace so that sometimes we do not know whether to giggle or scream. If his own admissions about the things that scare him are to be taken to heart then Spielberg exhibits real Everyman fears of elevators, air travel and the sea. Indeed, this Everyman quality is what invests his films with so much of their impact – in essence they are about the very people who watch them. Over the years, Spielberg's films have shifted from being about mothers caring for endangered and lost children (usually boys or even men) to fathers learning to care for sons (and sometimes daughters), whether literally (*Hook*) or more usually symbolically (*Empire of the Sun, Indiana Jones and the Temple of Doom, Always, Indiana Jones and the Last Crusade, Saving Private Ryan, Jurassic Park, Schindler's List, Amistad*).

In the mid-1980s Spielberg said that when he was fifty

he would be forgiven by the Hollywood establishment. For what he did not quite know but one assumes he meant forgiven for being so popular and, at that point, for working in very generic forms which were arguably not award-friendly. *Ghandi* won in 1982 for Best Picture (*ET* was nominated) but you might want to argue that ET is the more cinematic film.

Of course, nobody is infallible and Spielberg has received his fair share of criticism for his work – for being too sentimental (after *ET* some critics perceive his work taking a downturn), too facile (*Jurassic Park* and *Schindler's List* in the same year?), too focused on spectacle rather than substance, prone to happy endings no matter how traumatic the story and its stated claims to truth.

One of Spielberg's favourite American artists is Norman Rockwell, who was dismissed for many of the same reasons Spielberg has often been throughout his massively popular and iconic career. Whether it be a form of snobbery or simply a narrow outlook, there has been a never-ending tendency for the popular to be denied its potential for expression. Spielberg's is a total cinema in the way that Michael Powell and Emeric Pressburger's and Alfred Hitchcock's were (drawing on all techniques and technologies available) and as such there is a purity of its form and technique.

In more recent years Spielberg has moved away from the story settings and images that his name-making films often drew on. Yet, even now, almost thirty years into his career, Spielberg continues to populate his movies with Average Joes. And so, Captain Miller (a high-school teacher) in *Saving Private Ryan* is really not that far

14

removed from David Mann (a businessman) in *Duel*, Roy Neary (an electrician) in *Close Encounters of the Third Kind* and Martin Brody (a policeman) in *Jaws*.

Spielberg's movies have become their own vivid universe that people can quote from, refer to and remember – bound by the shared consciousness of cinema. As such, Spielberg confirms cinema's power to speak so richly and powerfully to so many.

Born on December 17 1946 in Cincinnati, Spielberg's childhood was fairly mobile, including time spent in Northern California and most famously Phoenix, Arizona. Countless interviews with him, especially up until *The Color Purple*, (although his interviews for *Saving Private Ryan* returned to the Phoenix years) testify to his time in Phoenix being when he discovered filmmaking, rapidly writing and directing his own short films, including *Escape to Nowhere* and most famously *Firelight*, his three-hour epic which he even managed to have screened locally at a cinema. In a 1985 interview with Time magazine and a piece of self-penned material, Spielberg explained how 'I dream for a living. I use my childhood and go back there for inspiration.' On more than one occasion, writings and responses to Spielberg's work reference the famous William Wordsworth line: 'The child is the father of the man.'

In his frequent focus on children and young people in his films, Spielberg has become the cinematic equivalent of that other American icon, Mark Twain, whose tall tales were peopled by essentially familiar down-to-earth characters.

Unlike many of his professional filmmaking contemporaries with whom he now almost mythically emerged alongside in the early 1970s, Spielberg was notable for having not attended film school. Instead he read English at Long Beach State in California whilst all the time beavering away at his own filmmaking projects. During this period, prior to his breakthrough with a contract to direct episodic television for Universal Studios, Spielberg met a filmmaker a few years older than himself called George Lucas, who had just completed his student film *THX 1138: Electronic Labyrinth* – later the basis for his debut feature *THX 1138* (1971). Spielberg has frequently referenced the impact of Lucas' student film on him, perhaps most notably as it alerted the budding director to the presence of others out there with as much filmmaking dexterity and finesse as himself. In 1969, Spielberg directed a short silent called *Amblin'*. It was his calling card, designed to demonstrate his facility with the craft and it got the young director into Universal. It was precisely this facility with craft that has frequently been both Spielberg's strength and apparent weakness. Look through the mountain of reviews of his films and one endlessly detects an admiration for his composition and fluid editing style but not for the so-called content.

Surely, though, the form is itself part of the content. They are not separate. The ideas and themes of a film are all too often mistaken for only being available through dialogue – testimony perhaps to the unfair hold that literature and theatre continue to hold over responses to film. Set design, camera placement, editing, sound, presence or absence of music – they all make up the meaning of a scene, of a sequence and finally of a movie. If it were only dialogue that was important then every film could just as easily exist as a radio play.

At the age of twenty-one, Spielberg found himself directing Hollywood great Joan Crawford in his first TV piece, an episode of *Night Gallery*, called *Eyes*. From all accounts, on the shoot for the show, Spielberg swiftly learnt that Hollywood is a relationship business. When you consider the pattern of Spielberg's career it seems fair to say that he has not only been a master manipulator of audience emotion but also of the business – 'the skulduggery of movie-making' as he once described it in one of his many infectiously energetic interviews.

In 1973, Universal screened a tele-movie called *Duel* based on a short story by Richard Matheson. Spielberg had directed it in 14 days and had mapped out the entire movie on a vast storyboard wall. The film was so successful that it was launched theatrically in Europe, notably in Britain where critic Dilys Powell gave it a very positive review. *Duel* is the story of a suburban man relentlessly and unfathomably pursued by a truck, seemingly possessed of a monstrous spirit. It was replete with visual power. Low on dialogue (never a bad thing for a film) and high on tension and atmosphere, the film secured Spielberg his first feature directing gig, *The Sugarland Express* (1974) starring Goldie Hawn. The film was not a commercial success yet it remains an intriguing film beyond the fact that it is Spielberg's first theatrical feature. Maybe its most significant long-term importance lies in it being the first film scored by John Williams who went on to become Spielberg's composer of choice and his most famous collaborator. Indeed, Williams' scores to Spielberg's films have become the sound of Spielberg, rather in the way that Bernard Herrmann's scores became the sound of Hitchcock, assuming a life beyond the films themselves. In his typically effusive liner notes to the Williams soundtracks for his films, Spielberg acknowledges the importance of this particular composer in transforming the material. Spielberg's other career-long collaborator has been the editor Michael Kahn. Editing is perhaps the one major film craft which has always failed to receive just recognition in mainstream media coverage of filmmaking. Kahn's work with Spielberg is a perfect case study in the impact of an editor. Since *Close Encounters*, their first collaboration, only once has Kahn not edited a Spielberg film and that was *ET*, which was edited by Carol Littleton (regular editor for director Lawrence Kasdan).

Through the 1970s and 1980s, Spielberg worked with a range of top cinematographers: Bill Butler, Dean Cundey, Allen Daviau and Vilmos Zsigmond. In the 1990s Spielberg has demonstrated a very rewarding relationship with cinematographer Janusz Kaminski, working with him on *Schindler's List, The Lost World: Jurassic Park, Amistad* and *Saving Private Ryan*. Kaminski has also lensed *AI*. It could be argued that the Kaminski collaboration symbolised Spielberg's second wind – the 1993 release of *Schindler's List* was seen by many to lift the director from a creative trough to a new and astounding peak. *Saving Private Ryan* again confirmed Spielberg's great skills and further enhanced his new-found role, as something of a Hollywood statesman and a history teacher for multiplex audiences around the world. For many, Spielberg suddenly seemed to become an artist – whilst for many others it only confirmed what had already been apparent in almost every movie he had made. Indeed, as many filmmakers testify, filmmaking is not an art but a craft, perhaps because it synthesises so many disciplines and tools. In an interview with Simon Hattenstone in The Guardian in September 1998, Spielberg commented: 'I've always thought of myself as a blue-collar director . . . I think an artist is somebody, to me, in the true sense of the word, someone who works alone, someone who has a direct rapport and deeply personal rapport with the subject . . . if I told stories that I could identify with as a person they would be very weird little experimental films. They wouldn't progress to a point then give you a reason to feel good about yourself, they would not pay off in the way you would expect them to coming from me.'

Like other Hollywood directors before him, because Spielberg made many films in very generic formats (horror, science fiction, adventure) he has perhaps not been seen as a serious filmmaker. Yet, his films are very smartly crafted. Sometimes critics rely on placing Spielberg's movies into a historical and social context or, even more dangerously, simply tying their storylines to the now widely-understood idea of mythological archetypes, to find some kind of all-important meaning in them. This is not necessarily the wrong way to respond, it's just that there are other ways. The release of Schindler's List is a clear example of a weighty subject matter being the source of people's respect for Spielberg rather than for the use and refinement of his craft which was as skilled and appropriate as it had been with the pulp adventure and thrills of Jaws and Raiders of the Lost Ark. The skill of a filmmaker (or any artist) is less in the subject matter they choose than in the way they treat it, the way they transcend it and give it their own particular view of the way the world is, could be or should be. Considering a film in full – everything you see in each shot, each sequence – is hopefully a rewarding way to respond to a movie, breaking down its elements to try and understand how the film creates its emotional effect on the audience. You don't direct a film by accident. By taking this approach to Spielberg's films we can see how he employs repeated stylistic approaches and story forms which in very broad terms, suggest he is telling the same story but with numerous refinements and variations.

To put it simply: Spielberg is a classic auteur – the author of his films, drawing together the many other creative voices involved in filmmaking so that one voice is heard. He is, as film critic Pauline Kael described him in her 1974 review of *The Sugarland Express*, a Howard Hawks for contemporary filmgoers. No matter what the subject or surface environment of a Spielberg film is (dusty 1930s adventure, dinosaur theme park, World War II, a future world of robots) there are certain shared themes, ideas and character configurations which tie the movies together – a consistency. As consistent, for example, as the work of his friend and colleague Martin Scorsese, whom Spielberg has often invoked as a figure to aspire to in terms of putting honest emotion up on the screen. (Although little has been heard about it for some time now, the two directors were supposed to be collaborating on a Western called *Into the Setting Sun*.)

For everything that Spielberg has been criticised for he

is equally applauded. He revived, with George Lucas, the adventure and science fiction genres – giving them both a new respectability. Since 1975 he has brought huge numbers of people to the movies. He charges his films with spectacle, wonder and emotion. He has made recent and traumatic historical watersheds known, and in some small way understood a little more clearly by many, especially the young. Just as Elvis had a cataclysmic impact on people in the 1950s so did Spielberg with his audiences, particularly between the mid-1970s and late 1980s. What Walt Disney was to Spielberg's generation, Spielberg became to the generation that grew up with his early films.

The Steven Spielberg of today is still predominantly a filmmaker but he also owns a film studio and his influence and aesthetic can be seen in the work of many other storytellers. The supernatural drama *The Sixth Sense* (1999) with its boy protagonist and sensitive adult engaging with extraordinary forces is very much a Spielberg kind of story. The film's director M Night Shyamalan has stressed how key to his decision to be a filmmaker his first viewing of *Raiders of the Lost Ark* was when he was kid. Interestingly, *The Sixth Sense* was produced by Spielberg's old collaborators, Frank Marshall and Kathleen Kennedy.

Amidst the spectacle, technical and technological grace of his films, Spielberg always invests them with a recognisable humanity. As he has always acknowledged, he is more often than not interested in the responses of an ordinary man (the kind who would go and see his films) to extraordinary circumstances which challenge, test and illuminate those who confront and become consumed by them. And yet, repeated viewing of Spielberg's films reveal that their most truly powerful moments are not the obviously astonishing ones, where the smoke and mirrors of film trickery and the real world meet but the quiet moments, away from the thunderous spaceships, duelling pirates, moon-jumping BMX bikes, rumbling trucks or the hail of gunfire. In collaboration with his screenwriters, Spielberg constructs big stories around very personal cores, each with a key moment of real human expression, often free of dialogue. A face looking or reacting is a key Spielberg image. Every Spielberg film has a core scene, the heart of the film's thought which lives on in the movie projectors of our minds. There are no fixed responses to any story in any form. Across the films that Steven Spielberg has directed there certainly seem to be enough recurring issues and motifs to suggest a consistent, thoughtful and significant storyteller at work.

What are these repeating elements then? At the heart of Spielberg's movies are issues of the imagination and of the individual attaining their heart's desire and a sense of belonging. Then too there are the relationships between sons and mothers, and fathers and sons (literally and figuratively). Spielberg has also always enjoyed dramatizing how an Everyman character responds to extraordinary pressures and circumstances. Faith in oneself and in the unseen and unknowable has fuelled several major Spielberg movies. Where would Indiana Jones be without a leap of faith at the end of his best adventure in *Indiana Jones and the Last Crusade*? Particular to many, but not all, of Spielberg's movies has been the challenge some characters have faced in truly growing up and acting selflessly and with newfound responsibility: *Always*, *Hook*, *Jurassic Park* and *Schindler's List* all address this notion, as their male protagonists learn to stop being selfish Peter Pan like figures.

It's fair to say that for many a so-called important subject is what makes a good film – which, in reality, is not always the case. The way in which the material is handled and crafted is what matters most.

For much of his early career Spielberg made movies set in essentially fantastic situations, so he was perhaps overlooked in terms of his dramatic skills and cinematic sensibility. In more recent years, having tackled stories set against more obviously important situations than treks for lost treasure and hungry sharks, Spielberg's rating as an artist (whatever that really means) has risen. Furthermore, Spielberg's adventures in so many genres allow him to cast himself as his favourite Hollywood filmmakers – for example, *Hook* can be seen as Spielberg in Vincente Minnelli and Victor Fleming (*The Wizard of Oz*) mode, *Jaws* is Spielberg as Alfred Hitchcock, *Saving Private Ryan* is Spielberg as Howard Hawks. *AI*, though more strikingly *Minority Report*, Stanley Kubrick – a fascinating convergence of very different sensibilities.

Spielberg has managed his career with great skill though he really does seem to have chosen directorial projects simply based on their pull as stories rather than as potentially popular ventures. In 2004, Spielberg's name is no longer absolutely synonymous with big thrills and fantasy stories. Spielberg now stands as a potential future pop-culture icon, alongside such fellow Americans as Mark Twain, Norman Rockwell, Walt Disney, Ernest

Hemingway and Aaron Copland. He is the most productive of his generation in terms of output and variety. In a 1997 article in Time about Spielberg's career, George Lucas had this to say about his pal and colleague: 'People like Steven don't come along every day. And when they do it's an amazing thing. It's like talking about Einstein or Tiger Woods. He's not in a group of filmmakers his age; he's far, far away.'

Primal Screen: The Monster Movies

Duel (1971)

Cast: Dennis Weaver (David Mann), Jacqueline Scott (Mrs Mann), Eddie Firestone (Cafe Owner), Lou Frizzell (Bus Driver), Carey Loftin (The Truck Driver)

Crew: Director: Steven Spielberg, Producer: George Eckstein, Screenplay: Richard Matheson, Cinematographer: Jack A Marta, Production Designer: Robert S Smith, Editor: Frank Morris, Music: Billy Goldenberg, 90 minutes

Story: David Mann is a middle-aged, Ordinary Joe – a suburban Everyman on a routine business trip who finds himself relentlessly menaced by an ominous truck, the driver of which Mann never sees. The film begins with Mann leaving his nondescript, suburban home and setting out in his nondescript car. Soon after, the truck makes itself known and begins its assault on Mann and his state of mind. Mann's composure fractures, convinced he is the victim of a maniacal truck driver. As Mann makes every effort to evade the truck he talks to himself to maintain and affirm his sanity. His sense of wellbeing heightens when he tells people of his plight and they do not believe him because the truck is never in evidence anywhere. The narrative concludes with Mann acting as inventively as he can in an attempt to survive the extraordinary experience. He leaps from his car which then plummets over a cliff top. The truck, going too fast, has no time to brake and crashes to its doom. Mann is safe – he has survived the duel.

Themes: An insular, routine life must eventually be challenged by an event out of the ordinary. In *Duel*, Spielberg announces one of his fundamental themes – the response of an ordinary person to an extraordinary circumstance. Tellingly, the ordinary hero ultimately emerges victorious from his life-threatening encounter, having attained a new level of understanding of himself and the wider world, and also having liberated emotions he had forgotten about. For all the suffering Mann endures it ultimately gives way to jubilation. *Duel* marks the start of a series of films directed by Spielberg which are set around narratives where frail humans are pursued by relentless beasts. In Duel, the beast is a mechanical, eighteen-wheel truck which is shot in such a way as to be anthropomorphised – a classic Spielberg technique which makes the inanimate seem alive. The windows of the truck are like eyes and the grille like a mouth. This beast is in a sense a Dark Angel – the trauma it induces is ultimately the redemption of the hero under attack. The hero is compelled to draw on his own mental, physical and emotional resources, is determined to survive the experience and hence ensure his freedom and future. *Duel* is also one of many Spielberg films to extract its Everyman hero from familiar, domestic surroundings and place him in an almost alien environment – in *Duel* the American desert and its lonely highways – in order to test him before returning him to his familiar, domestic world. Mann's very masculinity (in terms of bravery, resourcefulness) is tested. At the start of the film, his wife berates him for not 'defending' her from the advances of another man at a party. On the road, alone, Mann must protect himself from the advances of the truck.

Sound and Vision Keys: The rumbling of the truck acknowledges Spielberg's emerging flair for using sound, as well as the visual, to create menace (leap forward to 1998 and *Saving Private Ryan* and recall the rumbling, unseen tank as it approaches the soldiers in the bombed-out village). Spielberg creates a chaos of sound inside the car and around the truck which contrasts with the eerie silence of the desert. Mann wears glasses – a frequent signifier of the Spielberg hero, a somewhat fragile man with a somewhat intellectual nature perhaps. In a sense not a man's man. As Mann falls to his knees in the close of the film, there is a quasi-spiritual aspect to the image as he is silhouetted by the setting sun. Mann has been illuminated by the intensity of his experience from which he has been physically and emotionally released.

Background: Spielberg had already and would continue to direct television drama after Duel, including Savage (a precursor of sorts to Poltergeist), the first ever episode of Colombo, Marcus Welby and Owen Marshall. *Duel* was the demonstration of his skill. The film was released theatrically in Europe to rave reviews (notably Dilys Powell in Britain) and in part led to winning his first feature film a couple of years later. *Duel* was based on a short story by Richard Matheson. In preparing the film Spielberg storyboarded it completely, laying the images out on a huge wall. Check out Spielberg's use of long lenses to makes the truck appear nearer than it actually is. *Duel* marks the first of several Spielberg films where vehicles feature as key spaces in which characters must confront antagonistic forces. Spielberg said of the making of the film: '*Duel* was much more of a challenge [than *Jaws*], because trying to create that kind of fear out of a truck is a lot harder than the established fear of a man-eating fish underwater. But *Duel* had a whole new set of rules.' (Richard Combs, Primal Scream, Sight And Sound, 1977)

Verdict: Justly received as a stunning display of economical storytelling. *Duel* is useful in a way as being regarded as thumbnail sketch for the much larger scale 'monster movies' Spielberg went on to make. It contains the Spielbergian heroic archetype he elaborated upon, refined and enriched throughout his career – the character who has been abandoned and just wants to get home. An essential view – a prime example of Spielberg's self-dubbed world of mechanised madness. For many, *Duel* marked the start of Spielberg's best period of work – the 1970s. 5/5

Jaws (1975)

Cast: Roy Scheider (Brody), Robert Shaw (Quint), Richard Dreyfuss (Matt Hooper), Lorraine Gary (Ellen

Brody), Murray Hamilton (Mayor Vaughan), Carl Gottlieb (Meadows), Jeffrey Kramer (Hendricks), Peter Benchley (TV Interviewer)

Crew: Director: Steven Spielberg, Producers: Richard D. Zanuck, David Brown, Screenplay: Peter Benchley, Carl Gottlieb, Cinematographer: Bill Butler, Live Shark Footage: Ron & Valerie Taylor, Production Designer: Joseph Alves, Jr, Editor: Verna Fields, Special Effects: Robert A Mattey, Music: John Williams, 124 minutes

Story: Based on the best-selling novel *Jaws* by Peter Benchley, the feature film begins with the now iconic prelude where a young woman is attacked and killed by the eponymous shark, setting in motion the palpable tension and concern of a small coastal community, Amity, which depends on tourism for its trade. As paranoia grips the town, the new local police chief, Martin Brody, does all he can to keep things under control as he struggles to integrate into the town. When the shark attacks again, killing a boy, local concern reaches new levels. Brody allies with another newcomer, Matt Hooper, an ichthyologist interested in the shark reports. As the town grows increasingly desperate for the shark to be eliminated, a meeting is called and there the grizzled Quint makes himself known. He will find and kill the shark. The film's final movement sees Quint, Brody and Hooper on a fragile boat heading out to hunt the shark down. A tense and thrilling sea chase ensues which tests the men's bond and dependence on one another (a theme particularly evident later in *Amistad* and *Saving Private Ryan*) and also their own levels of resourcefulness and courage. Quint is killed. Hooper just about escapes. The anxious Brody slays the shark and returns to land with Hooper at his side as they float back home on a piece of debris.

Themes: Jaws's enduring message is that society must act together to overcome terror. Man is still very fragile in the face (and jaws) of nature and the unseen. The first of several Spielberg films to attain phenomenon status – the film transcending its form and speaking to very primal, universal fears and hopes about man's relationship to the wider, natural world. Jaws explores class prejudice to some degree – Quint's working-class dismissal of the middle-class intellectual, Hooper, (see the scene where Quint grabs Hooper's hands) in turn giving way to the recurrent Spielberg theme of masculinity coming under fire. The scar-comparing scene brilliantly distils this. At the end of the film it is Quint who dies, and the bespectacled Hooper and Brody (as far from a two-fisted, tough cop as you could expect) who survive.

The film plays, vividly, with the nature of fear – particularly the power of the unseen and unknown. The shark remained unseen partly because of the practicalities and problems with the fake shark – it looked fake. As a result this proved a blessing – the film works hard to suggest terror and is all the better for it. When we do glimpse the shark in all its glory we are shocked – witness the scene where Brody is facing camera talking to Hooper and Quint who are off camera. As Brody stands there the shark rises up out of the water. The boat becomes a microcosm of society where different temperaments and skills are pulled together in pursuit of a shared goal. As in *Duel,* the characters are tested by the very nature of their challenge away from the familiar world. They are abstracted and placed in a primal environment – the sea – where their sense of self is tested. Spielberg often portrays authority figures as figures of contempt, sometimes ineffectual and certainly out of tune with the more profound mysteries and powers that bind the heroes together as they struggle to recognise and fulfil their potential.

Brody is very much a child, insecure and slightly clumsy. Early on in the film he is shown tied up with the telephone wire (a sight gag repeated with the father in *Poltergeist*) and he matures through the course of the adventure. He is able to return home to his wife and children with a surer sense of his place and potential, having in a sense absolved himself of some of his limitations as a father than earlier in the story, notably his failure to protect his son who comes into close contact with the shark.

Sound and Vision Keys: Having begun his collaboration with composer John Williams the year before, their collaboration yields their first in a long line of themes which live beyond the film itself. Williams' kinetic, tense score is part horror, part adventure. The film is a near-perfect example of the impact of structure in yielding tension, rather than anything overtly graphic. Brody's home is very suburban, something of a fortress against the untameable, uncontrollable sea. Brody is put back in touch with his more primal roots. Quint's home/cabin is more primal, his shark jaws hung as trophies. We do not see where Hooper stays – he is a balance of the two men and is therefore most at home on the adventure. Hooper is the most boyish one; he sees it as play to some degree. Verna Fields' editing patterns invest the film with tension; the opening sequence is the perfect example. Bill Butler's cinematography captures the postcard quality of the coastal resort – its idyllic quality. Spielberg maximises the terror (sense of encroaching menace) by often placing the camera on the surface of the sea and frequently beneath, making us the shark. Most famously, perhaps, is the dolly zoom shot when Brody witnesses the shark attack. The background seems to explode as the camera tracks in, the lens zooming out through the tracking shot. Humour breaks tension and also gives it a perverse twist – for example the fake fin scene and also most famously the scar comparison scene and Quint's Indianapolis speech. The father/son aspect – Brody and his youngest boy mimicking one another – a trick that is repeated in *Close Encounters of the Third Kind*. This kind of tender pause from the tension is enough to invest the characters with recognisable emotion. In *Jurassic Park*, Spielberg employs the same device.

Background: Spielberg had not been approached to direct the film initially. He had picked up the manuscript of the novel before its publication and saw there was a movie idea in it. The original director always referred to the shark as a whale so he never got the job. Spielberg had considered Paul Newman and Sterling Hayden for the roles of Brody and Quint. On set, Dreyfuss and Shaw did have a slightly edgy relationship which clearly enriched their performances. The film was famously arduous – as most films that shoot at sea are. The schedule ran extensively over time and budget. The mechanical shark sunk to the seabed on one occasion.

Verdict: A Spielberg classic. The film that broke box-office records and secured his place as an A-list director. *Jaws* has been blamed for initiating the popcorn, juvenile mindset – blockbuster cinema and merchandising and the concept of the summer blockbuster movie. Three increasingly inferior sequels followed, none of which Spielberg had any involvement with. *Jaws* is notable for its fine balance between tension, spectacle and character. 5/5

Jurassic Park (1993)

Cast: Sam Neill (Dr Alan Grant), Jeff Goldblum (Ian Malcolm), Laura Dern (Dr Ellie Satler), Richard Attenborough (John Hammond), Bob Peck (Robert Muldoon),Martin Ferrero (Donald Gennaro), BD Wong (Dr Henry Wu), Joseph Mazzello (Tim Murphy), Ariana Richards (Lex Murphy), Samuel L Jackson (Ray Arnold), Wayne Knight (Dennis Nedry)

Crew: Director: Steven Spielberg, Producers: Kathleen Kennedy, Gerald R Molen, Lata Ryan (Associate Producer), Colin Wilson (Associate Producer), Screenplay: David Koepp, Michael Crichton, Production Designer: Rick Carter, Editor: Michael Kahn, Music: John Williams, Practical Effects: Michael Lantieri, Visual Effects: Dennis Muren (Industrial Light and Magic), Phil Tippett (Tippett

Studios), Stan Winston (Animatronic Dinosaurs), Michael
Lantieri (Physical Effects), 127 minutes

Story: Billionaire John Hammond has created a new kind
of theme park. Using DNA from fossilised dinosaurs,
Hammond's scientists have created a 'biological game
preserve' on an island off the coast of Costa Rica. To ensure
the safety and integrity of the park, called Jurassic Park,
Hammond invites two palaeontologists, Dr Alan Grant and
Dr Ellie Satler (who are partners), and Ian Malcolm, a
chaos mathematician, to spend a few days at the site. Also
present are Hammond's lawyer and Hammond's grandchildren, Tim and Lex. Upon arrival, Hammond's guests sight
a brachiosaur, across a vast plain and see dinosaurs drinking
at a lake. At the tour centre, the DNA extraction process is
explained and the guests voice concern over the ethics of
the process. On a motorised tour of the Tyrannosaurus Rex
area, a storm strikes and the island's electrical supply is cut
off. The vehicles are marooned and the children and Grant
are attacked by a T Rex. Malcolm is injured and returns to
the centre, where Hammond is relatively safe and desperate
to secure his grandchildren's safety. Drs Grant and Satler,
Ian Malcolm and the children are stranded in the jungle. A
dangerous, imperilled trek across the park back to some
kind of safety ensues, culminating with a showdown
between man and dinosaurs in the grand hall of the centre.
The humans only just survive and escape the island as the
dinosaurs once again rule the earth.

Themes: Man versus nature. *Jurassic Park* suggests a
caution and respect for nature's power. In the middle of

the film, the protagonists sit around a table and debate the ethics of the park's creation and work, and how dangerous science can be without a sense of responsibility. Spielberg, and his filmmaking team, strive and succeed in creating not movie monsters in the dinosaurs but animals existing in their natural habitat. Spielberg claimed Hatari (directed by Howard Hawks) was a key movie for him in the execution of the film. *Jurassic Park* celebrates community – look at the number of times Alan Grant references the group mentality of the dinosaurs – particularly when the gallimimus herd speeds dazzlingly into view over the ridge, sweeping Grant and the children up in their gallop.

Parenthood (guardianship) towards both the natural world and also towards one another is fundamental to the film. Just as in a movie as far back as *Indiana Jones and the Temple of Doom,* the male hero – wary about children and the need to protect them – is compelled to become a father figure and get the imperilled children safely through a dangerous experience. Grant's story arc sees him becoming the children's willing protector and he returns to a more primal, tender sense of fatherhood so that by the time he and the children fall asleep in the tree his arms are wrapped around them both. Spielberg lights the scene with a warm golden light. The film's closing image is of a flock of seabirds together – a family of birds as the mechanical bird (helicopter) lifts the survivors away from the ruined world of Jurassic Park. Grant smiles contentedly at his mate Ellie Satler, the children sitting with them – a family has been created, rather in the way that Indiana Jones finds himself a family man at the end of *Indiana Jones and the Temple of Doom.* Coming immediately after *Hook,*

Jurassic Park's espousal of fatherhood amidst the fantasy trappings is hardly a surprise. Like so many Spielberg male heroes, Grant moves beyond his own little professional world (playground) of gizmos and career to embrace a more compassionate life. This motif is repeated throughout so many Spielberg films – notably *Always, Hook, Indiana Jones and the Temple of Doom* and *Schindler's List.*

Throughout *Jurassic Park*, the character of Ian Malcolm repeatedly refers to chaos theory and the film's other key theme is how we can survive chaos and trauma by staying together. For all the creatures and spectacle, *Jurassic Park* is driven by a very human, elemental emotion –family and the desire to get back home. It is ultimately one more in Spielberg's ongoing narrative of rescue missions and quests to get back home.

Sound and Vision Keys: Spielberg's familiar bright lights and the inclusion of a rumbling soundtrack come into play from the first moment. In its opening shot the film's theme is encapsulated – a crate is thrust violently through the paradise like leaves of a forest. Mankind is destroying nature and the connection to their most natural impulses. Jurassic Park is Spielberg's green film. Like so many Spielberg heroes, the male hero is an intellectual more than a man of action. Grant wears a variation on Indiana Jones' trademark fedora and dresses in khaki trousers and a denim shirt – soft, inviting colours that complement the soft, inviting colours of Ellie Satler's clothes. Ellie is a classic Spielberg heroine – resourceful and strongwilled, but also very much in touch with nature and with a maternal instinct.

John Williams' now-famous main theme emphasises not the terror but rather the tenderness of the story, the sense of spectacle and of a great adventure. Spielberg demonstrates his enduring ability to ratchet up suspense in creative ways – notably the T Rex attack on the stranded trucks. We hear the creature before we see it; the glass of water vibrates on the dashboard. The key Spielberg image of people standing and watching and reacting with awe and often terror runs throughout the film.

Spielberg spikes terror with humour – just watch the blob of jelly shaking as the velociraptor shadow strikes the wall behind Tim. The family group shot – when Grant steps paternalistically between his partner and 'children' as the velociraptors close in.

Jurassic Park also contains one of the most sublime and historical moments in film history in which the reaction and emotion of the characters is absolutely fused with the emotions of the audience – when they first see the brachiosaur the characters' awe at the wonder of technology and nature is exactly what we feel sitting in the audience marvelling at the effect. And just to finesse the shot, Spielberg lays in a gently tracking wide shot. The film also is a textbook example of inter-cutting to create tension – the story goes back and forth between the T Rex attack and the complex, or between Tim on the fence and Ellie racing to turn the electrical power back on.

Background: Writer and filmmaker Michael Crichton wrote the novel Jurassic Park, inspired partly by observing his daughter's fascination with dinosaurs in the late 1980s. Spielberg expressed interest in the novel as a film property during a meeting with Crichton about a feature Spielberg was developing with him. That feature was called *ER*. A few years later it became the emotionally charged, smash hit TV series *ER*. William Hurt, Kurt Russell and Richard Dreyfuss were all approached for the role of Alan Grant. Originally, computer-generated dinosaurs were to be used minimally but as the film advanced the technology improved and the original plan was scrapped. Subsequently, visual-effects/stop-motion guru Phil Tippett (whose achievements include *Star Wars*, *The Empire Strikes Back*, *Return of the Jedi*, *Robocop* and *Starship Troopers*) found himself close to being out of a job.

However, he embraced the new digital horizon and fused computers and hands-on model animation to devise the Dinosaur Input Device which hooked up stop-motion models to computer-animation programming.

The film was completed twelve days ahead of schedule. Spielberg began shooting *Schindler's List* whilst *Jurassic Park* was still in production. George Lucas agreed to come in and supervise post-production and receives a special thanks credit at the close of the film. Jurassic Park marked Spielberg's second collaboration with ace fantasy film cinematographer Dean Cundey, giving the film a luxurious look. The film marks another collaboration between Spielberg and visual-effects supervisor Dennis Muren, after *ET: The Extra Terrestrial* and *Indiana Jones and the Temple of Doom*. When Stanley Kubrick saw *Jurassic Park* in 1993, he was very much encouraged to develop *AI* further. Muren supervised effects on *AI*.

Richard Attenborough was originally going to play Tootles in *Hook*. When Spielberg was unable to secure him for that role, Attenborough was Spielberg's first choice for Hammond. *Jurassic Park* was originally due to end with the humans defeating the velociraptors with machines.

Verdict: Not classic Spielberg but certainly an effective demonstration of the dovetailing of spectacle and genre forms with Spielberg's more personal concerns. Significant perhaps mostly for its contribution to the development of visual effects. 3/5

The Lost World: Jurassic Park (1997)

Cast: Jeff Goldblum (Ian Malcolm), Julianne Moore (Dr Sarah Harding), Pete Postlethwaite (Roland Tembo), Arliss Howard (Peter Ludlow), Richard Attenborough (John Hammond), Vince Vaughan (Nick van Owen), Vanessa Lee Chester (Kelly Malcolm), Peter Stormare (Dieter Stark), Harvey Jason (Ajay Sidhu), Richard Schiff (Eddie Carr), Thomas E Duffy (Dr Robert Burke)

Crew: Director: Steven Spielberg, Producers: Bonnie Curtis (Associate Producer), Kathleen Kennedy (Executive Producer), Gerald R Molen, Colin Wilson, Screenplay: Michael Crichton, David Koepp, Cinematographer: Janusz Kaminski, Production Designer: Rick Carter, Editor: Michael Kahn, Music: John Williams, 129 minutes

Story: It is several years after the first visit to Jurassic Park on Isla Nublar. Ian Malcolm, his career on the ropes after the first Jurassic Park experience, is summoned to visit John Hammond who explains about the existence of another island, Isla Sornar on which live dinosaurs without any boundaries. Hammond explains that a palaeontologist named Sarah Harding is already on the island documenting the creatures. Harding is Malcolm's girlfriend. Incensed at Hammond's hubris, Malcolm sets off to the island along with a video documentarian named Nick van Owen and an engineer/technologist named Eddie Carr. Unbeknownst to Malcolm, his daughter Kelly stows away. Upon arrival on the island, Ian reunites with his partner – amidst rampaging stegosaurs.

Soon the group finds itself engaged in a battle for survival as it challenges a group of animal hunters who have arrived with the intention of capturing a T Rex. Malcolm, Harding and Van Owen first let loose those dinosaurs that have been captured by the hunters then tend to a baby T Rex in their mobile study unit which is violently attacked by two T Rexes, fiercely protective of their young. With communications and facilities rapidly declining, and with hunters being picked off by the dinosaurs, the heroes and the 'villains' must overcome their differences and band together to reach an abandoned communications centre from where they can call for help. Roland Tembo, ace game hunter, succeeds in tranquillising a T Rex, which is taken to San Diego to be the main attraction at Jurassic Park: San Diego. The narrative climaxes with our heroes racing to the mainland, where the T Rex breaks free of its storage hold and rampages through the suburbs at night as Malcolm and Harding race against time to retrieve the T Rex baby and use it to lure the T Rex mother back to the ship. The film's villain is dispatched by the T Rex and *The Lost World* ends with

Malcolm, Harding and Kelly watching John Hammond on the news saying how nature must be left alone.

The last image is a panoramic shot of dinosaurs grazing on an island as, rather ominously, a pterodactyl swoops in, lands on a tree and with the sun throwing it into silhouette, screeches menacingly.

Themes: A more Spartan, darker film than *Jurassic Park*, *The Lost World* expresses a world of devastation – a kind of Jurassic apocalypse in which, as Spielberg and screenwriter David Koepp acknowledged on the film's release, the central drama was between the compulsion to hunt and the compulsion to protect. Nature again is all-powerful.

When the stegosaurs attack Sarah Harding early in the film as she photographs one of their young, she shouts out to Ian 'They're just protecting their baby,' to which Malcolm, running to rescue her shouts, 'So am I.' The heroes are the nurturing, protective force, the villains the big game hunters and InGen corporation. At the very end of the film, John Hammond states: 'If we can step aside and trust in nature life will find a way.' Ian Malcolm is the film's protagonist and, as with Grant in the first film, is transformed; he connects with his paternal instinct when his daughter tags along for the adventure. Early in the film, Spielberg focuses very heavily, through dialogue, on Ian's comically uneasy relationship with his daughter who chastises him for not being a good father. 'I'm your daughter all the time you know. You can't just abandon me whenever opportunity knocks,' she says. As with Alan Grant in *Jurassic Park*, the adventure compels Malcolm to draw on his primal compulsion to protect his young. Spielberg once again expresses the inadequacy of the modern world in the face of nature through a tense, volatile action sequence – this time a scientific caravan is imperilled by two T Rexes when a baby Rex is taken in by the scientist. Once more, heavy rainfall compounds the tension as the caravan is edged over a cliff. In one of Spielberg's most tense action scenes, Sarah Harding falls and lands on the window at the back of the caravan which is now facing straight down to the sea and rocks. As she lies on the glass it begins to crack like ice.

Sound And Vision Keys: Spielberg's first film after *Schindler's List*, he employs a lot of hand-held camera work, not only on smaller scenes but even during the massive game hunt sequence, for example, which lends the action an immediacy and edginess. Torchlights cutting violently through the darkness evoke *ET* particularly. As in *Jurassic Park*, Spielberg makes purely visual allusions to man's rape of the land and of nature during a dinosaur hunt. Nature's lethal cunning is best visualised in an overhead shot when three raptors cut through high grass rather like sharks (or torpedoes) through water before downing several intruders.

Background: A follow-up to the first *Jurassic Park* was inevitable. Unfortunately, *The Lost World* lacks the sense of magic and wonder that *Jurassic Park* possessed, in part though this is due to the premise – a lost, ravaged world. Once again Dennis Muren, Michael Lantieri and Stan Winston supervised computer, animatronic and practical effects. Spielberg's camera is free to roam, giving it a vérité, documentary feel. *The Lost World* also represented Spielberg's final contractual directorial commitment to Universal.

Verdict: Arguably, the only boring film Spielberg has ever made – as you watch the film you feel that it was not particularly engaging material to work with. The film ignited the box office but failed to ignite much passion in the audience. Spielberg's weakest film. 2/5

Awfully Big Adventures:
The Indiana Jones Series

Raiders of the Lost Ark (1981)

Cast: Harrison Ford (Indiana Jones), Karen Allen (Marion Ravenwood), Paul Freeman (Rene Belloq), John Rhys Davies (Sallah), Ronald Lacey (Toht), Denholm Elliot (Marcus Brody), Alfred Molina (Satipo), Wolf Kahler (Dietrich), Anthony Higgins (Gobler), Vic Tablian (Barranca/Monkey Man), Don Fellows (Colonel Musgrove), William Hootkins (Major Eaton), Frank Marshall (Pilot)

Crew: Director: Steven Spielberg, Producers: Howard Kazanjian, Robert Watts, Frank Marshall, George Lucas (Executive Producer), Screenplay: Lawrence Kasdan, Cinematographer: Douglas Slocombe, Production Designer: Norman Reynolds, Editor: Michael Kahn, Music: John Williams, Special Visual Effects: Industrial Light and Magic, 115 minutes

Story: The South American jungle, 1936, and archaeological adventurer, Professor Indiana Jones, approaches a temple with a band of guides. After surviving numerous

45

booby traps and retrieving the treasure, Jones is confronted by his arch rival, Rene Belloq, who snatches the golden idol from him. Jones returns to the States and his university where he is charged with a mission from the US government – retrieve the Lost Ark from Egypt before the Nazis do. Jones is initially reluctant but is finally convinced and sets out on his mission. His first stop is Nepal where he reunites with an old flame, the tough talking Marion Ravenwood.

Together they travel to Egypt where Jones locates his old friend Sallah. The real search for the Ark now begins and it is a race against time. Jones locates the treasure in an incredible temple and once again has it stolen away by Belloq. Jones overcomes much resistance in pursuit of the Ark, notably in a dazzling truck chase. Finally, he and Marion are taken prisoner and the Nazis and Belloq open the Ark, hoping to find inside it the tablets engraved with The Ten Commandments. Instead, they unleash the wrath of God and are destroyed. Indiana and Marion are spared and return to the States where The Ark is locked away in a vast warehouse. Jones and Ravenwood walk off together, arm in arm.

Themes: Indiana Jones represents independence and a maverick sensibility – single and without children he roams the world in search of adventure. Jones also represents what has become a familiar Spielberg type – the man who never quite grows up and who goes on some illuminating adventure beyond the real world only to return the (emotionally) richer for it. Jones has a dual identity – mild-mannered teacher and two-fisted adventurer who is frustrated by bureaucracy. Indiana Jones is a very human hero, afraid of snakes and visibly demonstrative of his emotions. When he gets hit we see the pain on his face. The adventure he undergoes could be seen to enrich his life as he steps away from his mundane teaching job and steps out into the wider world where, as in all adventure stories, the key issue is of performance, of the hero being up to the task before them. Jones experiences the value of friendship and solidarity. The Ark represents the power in the world of the unknown and unseen. Throughout Spielberg's movies there has been a sense of a spectral power which sometimes acts malevolently but frequently benignly towards the characters. At the end of *Raiders*, Jones and Ravenwood are saved because they do not look at the power of the Ark – they respect its strength. A large part of Indy's appeal is in his determination and persistence. He is a truly heroic character because of his tenacity and not his physical ability or toughness. As an adventure film, meaning is communicated almost completely through action. What the characters do is what they are and hence what they mean. *Raiders*, like all the Indiana Jones films, ends with an affirmation of non-materialism and the damnation of greed. Marion waits for Indy on the steps of the government building – perhaps she is the real treasure.

Sound and Vision Keys: Sunlight as symbolic of illumination. Tracking shots to draw us directly into the action and environments. In the truck chase Spielberg crafts one of the finest action sequences ever because it is tied to consistent character behaviour. Throughout the film, but notably during the map room sequence, natural light symbolises illumination and understanding. The old man who decodes the medallion for Indy is synonymous with stargazing and wisdom.

John Williams created a score and now-legendary main theme that, like so many of his other works, has become part of the residue of pop culture, brimming with a mix of courage and energy. It is a theme for adventure in the broadest sense – for being out in the world, for being active and bold. Indiana Jones is a very strong character, iconic above and beyond his adventures.

Background: Director of *THX 1138*, *American Graffiti* and *Star Wars*, George Lucas conceived of Indiana Jones in the early 1970s as he was developing *Star Wars*. Bringing writer Philip Kaufman aboard, Lucas refined the concept and Kaufman provided the context of the Ark. However, it was only in the late 1970s that Lucas finally got the ball rolling in what has now become Hollywood folklore. Escaping Hollywood in late May 1977 when *Star Wars* premiered, Lucas holidayed with his pal Steven Spielberg and sitting on the beach together building sandcastles Lucas pitched the project to Spielberg who had said he wanted to direct a James Bond film. Lucas said he had something better in his archaeologist hero. An agreement was made, and three years later the film was in production. Lawrence Kasdan, a new writer, was brought in to write the screenplay based on Lucas and Kaufman's story and between Lucas, Spielberg and Kasdan a script was generated. Tom Selleck was initially going to be cast. Craig T Nelson, the dad from

Poltergeist, and Peter Coyote, Keys the scientist in *ET*, were also considered. However, when Selleck could not be released from his TV contract to play *Magnum*, Lucas and Spielberg turned to Harrison Ford despite Lucas' initial reluctance to return to an actor with whom he had worked, albeit very successfully, before. Spielberg and Lucas made a deal with Paramount Pictures. The film was shot over the summer of 1980 in Tunisia, London (at Elstree Studios, the old *Star Wars* stomping ground) and Hawaii. Even the foliage from *The Empire Strikes Back's* Dagobah set were pulled out of storage and used to festoon the South American temple interiors at the start of *Raiders* .It was released in June 1981 and became a huge hit. Many critics thrilled to it but some loathed it as a very mechanical exercise in kinetic filmmaking. Perhaps the unrelenting energy of the film was its main idea. Perhaps, in a sense, the form was the content. The film's success led to two sequels, both of which enriched the Indiana Jones format (a fourth film in the series is currently in the works, see the final chapter).

The prevailing criticism of the Indiana Jones films has been their possibly unthinking racism towards non-white cultures.

Indiana Jones was originally named Indiana Smith but apparently Spielberg thought the name Smith too common. The film's opening shot mirrors the opening shot in the Akira Kurosawa film Yojimbo.

Verdict: For many one of the high-water marks in adventure cinema and voted one of the best American films of all time. 4/5

Indiana Jones and the Temple of Doom (1984)

Cast: Harrison Ford (Indiana Jones), Kate Capshaw (Willie Scott), Ke Huy Quan (Short Round), Amrish Puri (Mola Ram), Roshan Seth (Chattar Lal), Philip Stone (Captain Blumburtt), Roy Chiao (Lao Che), David Yip (Wu Han)

Crew: Director: Steven Spielberg, Producers: Kathleen Kennedy, Robert Watts, Frank Marshall, George Lucas, Screenplay: Willard Huyck, Gloria Katz, Story: George Lucas, Cinematographer: Douglas Slocombe, Production Designer: Elliot Scott, Editor: Michael Kahn, Music: John Williams, Visual Effects: Industrial Light and Magic, 118 minutes

Story: Shanghai, 1935. Indiana Jones, dressed in a white tuxedo, enters a swish nightclub as an elaborate dance finishes. He seats himself opposite several Chinese men led by the villainous Lao Che and presents them with a jade casket containing the ashes of some great Chinese figure. When Jones asks for his payment, trouble ensues and he is drugged by the gangsters. With glamorous nightclub singer Willie Scott at his side, Indy escapes with the assistance of his plucky little helper, the boy Short Round. Soon, Indy, Willie and Short Round are on a plane – piloted by Lao Che's henchmen. The plane takes off and Indy is convinced of his victorious escape. Shortly after, Indy, Willie and Short Round leap from the plane as it careens towards a mountaintop. Our heroes arrive at an impoverished, famine-stricken village whose protecting Sankara stones are gone. Indy, Willie and Short Round are regarded as gods, having fallen from the sky. Against his wishes, and despite his protestation, Indy is charged with retrieving the village's Sankara stones. The village's children have been stolen by evil tyrant Mola Ram who is using them in his mines to dig for the last Sankara stone with which he can rule the world. Indy agrees to the mission and sets off to recover the stone with no thought at this stage of rescuing the children. He soon stumbles upon The Temple of Doom, packed with hundreds of chanting men and presided over by a menacing statue of Kali. When a vicious sacrificial ceremony ends, Indy goes to retrieve the stones. About to bag them he hears the screams of children and watches hundreds of children slaving away for the third Sankara stone. He is captured and handed over to Mola Ram. Willie and Short Round are also captured and after a dazzling escape Willie, Short Round and Indy lead the slave children to freedom. A final showdown between Indy and Mola Ram is duked out on a rope bridge and cliff face. Indy wins, but only just. Indy, Willie and Short Round return to the village with the surviving Sankara stone and the village's children. Indy and Willie kiss as Short Round looks on.

Themes: For all its genre trappings, *Temple of Doom* anticipates a theme and narrative motif which occupied much of Spielberg's work in the 1990s – the role of the father figure in rescuing and restoring a family, whilst also learning to move beyond material gain. Indiana rescuing the children from slavery is not so very different from

Oskar Schindler rescuing the Jews from the concentration camp. In this film, Indiana Jones becomes something of a family man, gaining both a partner and a son. At his lowest point, disconnected from his real self, Indiana is saved by Short Round's love for him and breaks the spell that Indy is under. Indy's relationship with Willie is more flirtatious than his relationship with Marion. The film suggests that compassion is its own reward – Indy's adventure truly begins when he hears the screams of the children. Once again, his experiences reveal new aspects of the world to him. As in so many Spielberg films, the child is rendered more canny and competent than the adult.

Sound and Vision Keys: The starry sky ushers in the adventures as Indy tells Short Round that they are going in search of 'Fortune and glory, kid, Fortune and glory.' In a sense Indy is himself an actor as he enters into adventurer mode whenever he dons his fedora. Willie is a nightclub singer for whom a world less fussy and more chaotic than the one she is used to is a challenge. The chaos of the world is made more negotiable by the team sticking together – a motif we see elaborated on in *Jurassic Park*. The stunt scenes feel more like dance numbers, especially the escape from the mine before getting to the mine cars. Williams' score only enhances the rhythms. The action is far more silent film orientated and Spielberg applies a dose of well-judged visual comedy to the material – in a sense evoking *1941* but with far more control. Douglas Slocombe's cinematography brings out the exotic Asian landscape and also uses reds and shadows to suggest the horror of the Temple of Doom.

Background: The screenplay was written by Lucas' old collaborators Willard Huyck and Gloria Katz, with whom he wrote *American Graffiti*, and who contributed several importantly witty and human lines of dialogue to the original *Star Wars* film. Dan Aykroyd is the stuffy chap in shorts who leads Indy to the plane at the aerodrome and the figures in pith helmets in the background are George Lucas and Steven Spielberg. The film's intensity resulted in the creation of the PG 13 rating in America.

Verdict: *Temple of Doom* has an exuberance and refreshing darkness to it. Interesting as a precursor to themes Spielberg will explore more vigorously in the ensuing years. Pauline Kael's review of the film may yet be the most enthusiastic for it. 3/5

Indiana Jones and the Last Crusade (1989)

Cast: Harrison Ford (Indiana Jones), Sean Connery (Professor Henry Jones), Alison Doody (Elsa Schneider), Denholm Elliot (Marcus Brody), John Rhys Davies (Sallah), Julian Glover (Walter Donovan), River Phoenix (Young Indy), Michael Byrne (Vogel), Kevork Malikyan (Kazim), Robert Eddison (Grail Knight), Richard Young (Fedora), Alexei Sayle (Sultan), Alex Hyde-White (Young Henry Jones), Paul Maxwell (Panama Hat)

Crew: Director: Steven Spielberg, Producer: Robert Watts, Executive Producers: Frank Marshall, George Lucas, Screenplay: Jeffrey Boam, Production Designer: Elliot

Scott, Cinematographer: Douglas Slocombe, Music: John Williams, Editor: Michael Kahn, Visual Effects: Industrial Light and Magic, 127 minutes

Story: Utah, 1912. Indiana Jones is a Boy Scout and he stumbles upon a band of grave robbers stealing the legendary Cross of Coronado from a native American cave. Seized by a sense of moral obligation, Indiana snatches the treasure when the robbers' backs are turned – he intends to take it to a museum. A frantic, comic chase ensues on horseback and then on a circus train as Indy escapes. He tries to explain to his father what has ensued but he is silenced. The local sheriff arrives and ensures that Indy hands the Cross of Coronado over to the robbers. In return the lead robber gives Indy his fedora. Cut to the Portuguese Coast, 1938, and Indiana Jones is a grown man still in pursuit of the Cross. This time he retrieves it in a swashbuckling moment, leaping from a ship to safety just as it explodes and sinks, taking the grave robbers' leader with it. Back at his university Indy is taken to the apartment of Walter Donovan, art lover and collector. Donovan shows Jones part of a stone tablet relating to the Holy Grail, and informs Indy that his father, esteemed Grail scholar, Henry Jones has been kidnapped by the Nazis in their search for the sacred cup. With his friend and colleague, Marcus Brody, Indy sets out to find his father, via an encounter with Elsa Schneider in Venice. A series of double-crosses (including Walter Donovan revealing his Nazi sympathies) and attempts on Indy's life lead him to Brunwald Castle where he finds his father being held prisoner by the Nazis. Indy and his father escape the castle and head for Iskenderun where they meet up with Indy's pal Sallah and the trail for the Grail moves towards its climax. Henry and Marcus are captured by the Nazis and then rescued by Indy before they finally reach the Grail Temple. Henry Jones is shot by Donovan who orders Indy to go and retrieve the Grail. Indy survives several traps and arrives in a beautiful chamber where the Grail rests under the watchful gaze of an ancient and frail Grail Knight. Donovan and Schneider's greed gets the better of them when they seize the wrong cup, the most ornate one. Donovan drinks from the false Grail and perishes. Indy chooses the correct Grail and returns to his father, healing his wound with water from the cup. The temple begins to collapse and the cup is dropped. Elsa grasps for it and perishes too, and the cup is lost to nature. Indy, Sallah, Marcus and Henry escape and the Grail Knight waves farewell. Our heroes ride into the sunset.

Themes: Lawrence Kasdan, in a 1994 interview with Graham Fuller in a volume of the annual film digest Projections (Volume 6, published by Faber And Faber), commented that the Grail story is 'hugely powerful to Steven, and he sees most of his movies that way.'

The Last Crusade is a rescue story in both surface, plot terms (retrieving Indy's father and retrieving the Grail) and also in emotional terms (father and son rescue one another at an emotional level and heal the wound of estrangement between them). In The Last Crusade the son rescues the father by helping him realise a dream and the father rescues the son by acknowledging his son's chosen identity – at the very end of the story Jones Senior can no longer keep calling his son Junior but instead acknowledges him by the name Indiana. At that moment, Indy realises the physical Grail is meaningless. He and his father have found the treasure between themselves and the material world fades into insignificance. This tender, unexpected and brilliant moment builds on the warmth developed between the two across the film, amidst their bickering. The story charts a quest and compulsion to attain a goal – Jones Senior is driven by an obsession for the Grail which matches Roy Neary's obsession to see the UFOs in *Close Encounters of the Third Kind*. As often the case with comedy though (and make no mistake *Indiana Jones and the Last Crusade* is a highly assured comedy adventure) the seriousness of its themes are overshadowed by the happy-go-lucky tone. The film reflects on the nature of heroism – it is not to be found in physical strength or bravery but in tenacity and determination – the very essence of Indiana Jones. In the same year as *The Last Crusade*, Spielberg's other feature *Always* also concerned itself with heroism. The film promotes respect for knowledge and wisdom and also suggests that those without some faith in themselves and in unseen forces can perish. In *The Last Crusade* the hero endures and survives because of what you might call the angel on their shoulders. Indy is framed twice with a lion (symbolic of courage) statue above him, as though looking protectively over him.

Sound and Vision Keys: *The Last Crusade* is the most motif-laden of the series. First, its opening sequence explains in very archetypal ways the Indiana Jones character. His facial scar is explained as is the use of the bullwhip, the fear of snakes and the wearing of the trademark fedora. Perhaps the key line in the film and for the whole series is when the robber who gives Indy his fedora says, 'You lost today kid but that doesn't mean you have to like it.' *The Last Crusade* is, by the nature of its plot, tied to Christian imagery, notably of the lion and the crucifix. Spielberg's framing is very clear and always advances the narrative. At Henry Jones' ransacked home, Indy is framed in close-up, a Grail painting on the wall behind him. The lion on the circus train, the lion carvings in the library, and in the temple. The motif of illumination and a way of seeing is presented verbally and visually, especially at the end of the movie when Indy makes his leap of faith. For example, look how dominant the library's stained-glass window is when Indy arrives at the library in Venice. As much as is possible amidst the chaos of a big-budget B-movie, the film follows the illumination of Indy and Henry towards themselves and one another. The film demonstrates how history can illuminate us. Henry Jones even quotes Charlemagne and in doing so lends a flourish to a moment of inspiration that saves him and his son from impending doom.

In this third film, the role of visual effects is not as extensive or overt as in the previous two films but when they are employed they work with simple power because of the emotion and drama underpinning them. Throughout the film, Spielberg visualises and makes concrete the film's ideas.

The classic Spielberg theme of communication also becomes part of the film at a climactic moment. With Henry shot and bleeding to death Indy must go alone to retrieve the Grail yet remains in touch with his dad almost telepathically. So their relationship has an almost magical quality, rather like the relationship between Celie and Nettie *in The Color Purple* and between ET and Elliot in *ET: The Extra Terrestrial*.

Background: Shot in 1988, Spielberg has acknowledged his compulsion to make a brighter film than *Temple Of Doom*. The film almost feels like one big lark in a very infectious way. *The Last Crusade* is certainly the most light-hearted and literate of the three Indy films. Inevitably, numerous concepts were discussed in the movie's script development – including one that would have had something of a haunted house aspect to it and another involving a Monkey King scenario in Africa. Lucas' conception for Henry Jones was originally for a far more bookish, less physical presence but Spielberg pushed for someone who would be a screen equal for Harrison Ford – enter Sean Connery. Tom Stoppard (who had written the screenplay for *Empire of the Sun*) was brought in to fine-tune the script. Julian Glover who portrays Donovan appeared as General Veers in *The Empire Strikes Back* commanding an ATAT walker.

Verdict: One of the strongest films of Spielberg's career. A true adventure classic combining laughs, gasps and heart. As of this writing, Lucas, Spielberg and Ford are developing a fourth Indiana Jones film (see final chapter).

For a spectacular action comedy movie, the film's real satisfaction comes not in its stunts and huge scale but in its emotional drive and intelligence. 5/5

To Fly

ET: The Extra Terrestrial (1982)

Cast: Dee Wallace Stone (Mary), Henry Thomas (Elliot), Peter Coyote (Keys), Robert McNaughton (Michael), Drew Barrymore (Gertie), KC Martel (Greg), Sean Frye (Steve), C Thomas Howell (Tyler), Erika Eleniak (Pretty Girl), Richard Swingler (Science Teacher), Pat Walsh/Debra Winger (ET voice, uncredited) Crew: Director: Steven Spielberg, Producers: Kathleen Kennedy, Steven Spielberg, Melissa Mathison (Associate Producer), Screenplay: Melissa Mathison, Cinematographer: Allen Daviau, Production Designer: James D Bissell, Editor: Carol Littleton, Music: John Williams, ET Designed by Carlo Rambaldi, Special Visual Effects: Dennis Muren, Industrial Light and Magic, 115 minutes

Story: A forest at night. A spaceship like a big Christmas bauble sits mysteriously in the forest. The ship's crew of alien creatures rummage through the foliage. The visitors' chests glow red and suddenly the peace of the forest is destroyed by invasive car headlights and screeching wheels – a team of scientists have arrived. All of the aliens board the ship, except one who is pursued by the humans. It escapes. A couple of nights later and the ET is hiding out close to a suburban back garden. A young boy named Elliot discovers the creature and takes him in and they begin to bond. Elliot soon introduces ET to his brother and sister swearing them to secrecy and not to tell their mother. Elliot and ET's friendship deepens and they connect with one another so powerfully that they share feelings and thoughts. Slowly but surely, the scientists close in around Elliot's home. ET builds a device to communicate with his distant family so that they return and take him home. ET begins to weaken and scientists invade Elliot's house. Elliot's health deteriorates too. The home becomes a makeshift hospital and laboratory as ET and Elliot are hooked up to monitors and medication. ET goes into cardiac arrest and apparently dies. Elliot recovers and discovers that his alien pal is still alive. An escape plan is hatched and Elliot and his friends join together and take ET back to the woods to rejoin his returning family. Elliot and ET must finally say goodbye as the spaceship touches back down in the forest. ET says goodbye and boards the ship, which rockets away leaving a rainbow trail across the starry sky.

Themes: Love is the big idea in this film with its emphasis on compassion and tolerance. This is the first of Spielberg's movies to resound with a plea for tolerance towards strangers and outsiders. ET becomes a surrogate father and friend to Elliot whose father in the story has divorced his mother. The film celebrates the sanctuary that childhood can sometimes offer whilst also acknowledging the rougher side of being a kid. Suburbia is shown positively as a protective cocoon, not as a potentially boring and stifling environment. As many have noted, *ET* is Spielberg's hymn to the suburbs. The film's drama is driven largely by the main character's faith and desire to return home. ET is an angelic character who foreshadows the gentle and lost Cinque in *Amistad*. Like *Close Encounters of the Third Kind*, *ET* is about communication and how it can exist across space and time. As in some of Spielberg's other films, adults are shown to misjudge the central situation whilst the children and young people are able to understand it completely, deal with the extraordinary circumstances correctly and with invention and courage. There is a real melancholy to the story in the form of Elliot's loneliness and ET's burning wish to phone home. In *ET* this familiar Spielberg theme becomes crystallised and more powerful than in any of his previous films. The film charts Elliot's emotional growth; he goes from being a slightly clumsy kid to being very mature. By the end of the movie Elliot has found his true self, just as other Spielberg heroes find their true selves through the course of their often extraordinary adventures.

ET is Spielberg's great suburban epic about looking for belonging, and is still probably Spielberg's boldest statement of his key theme of loneliness.

Sound and Vision Keys: The starry sky as the harbinger of hope, magic and adventure. Flight makes its strongest impression in *ET* as an expression of freedom and escape; of a healthy release from everyday life. Through this image, Spielberg uses an ancient image to charge his contemporary fairy-tale. Allen Daviau's cinematography lends the entire film a soft, magical quality and throughout sunlight frequently lights rooms – particularly the walk-in cupboard where there is a circular stained-glass window in the background. Late in the film, Spielberg invokes a sense of the halo when he frames ET and Elliot through the circular perplex of the icebox that the presumed dead ET is stored in. Soon after we see the rescued ET standing in the back of the ambulance with a blanket draped around him, his heart glowing – there is something undeniably religious about the feeling this image carries. You could even say that the setting sun, as Elliot and his friends cycle in front of it, serves as a symbol of life, energy and hope.

What lends the film its believability is the fact that Spielberg chooses to frame ET and the human performers in the same shot throughout so that the scenes carry a naturalistic pace which draws the audience in. Because he does not cut to a close-up on ET every time ET does something we begin to forget he is an effect. Just witness the scene shot in silhouette where Elliot talks to ET about his toys and fish. The skill with which Carlo Rambaldi designed ET and the skill with which he was operated on set clearly gave Spielberg maximum opportunity to have ET interact with the children.

As in *Close Encounters of the Third Kind* and the *Jurassic Park* films, science is presented as an invasive force which is foiled by a basic sense of decent behaviour, notably the instinct to protect.

In many Spielberg films, a memento is passed between protagonists at the end of the film. In *ET* it is the potted flower which revives to full colour when ET comes back to life. Less tangibly, the memento ET leaves with Elliot is the touch to the forehead and the empowering statement,

'I'll be right here.' Memory is a virtually intravenous emotional line through Spielberg's films – ET wants Elliot to know he will not be forgotten. Elliot's red-hooded top evokes Little Red Riding Hood, giving it a fairy-tale aspect and also tapping into other colour associations, notably of red equating to sacrifice and life. Spielberg uses jump-cuts twice in the film – first for Elliot's initial face-to-face encounter with ET and then when Elliot shuts his eyes whilst riding just before the bikes vault sky-ward. The effect is jarring and very simply heightens a sense of drama – of tension and suspense.

Toys are photographed in such a way as to seem some-where close to living and breathing – the whole idea of the world as having some other potential. Even the adult Keys tells Elliot that he has been waiting since he was ten for an alien to come to earth and then says that he found Elliot first. Keys connects with Elliot whilst the other adults act aggressively towards him and his friends, notably the armed police forming their blockade.

Throughout the film Spielberg uses the security of a well-furnished middle-class suburban home to evoke a real warmth – on two key occasions, when ET and Elliot watch Gertie having Peter Pan read to her and secondly when Michael curls up in the cupboard as ET lies dying downstairs. The Peter Pan reference expands and clarifies the film's commitment to the idea of the importance of faith, trust, innocence and youth.

Background: Spielberg conceived a refined concept for *ET* (initially titled *A Boy's Life*) in 1980 during the shoot for *Raiders Of The Lost Ark*. He then developed it further with Melissa Mathison (who had written the script for ace kid's film *The Black Stallion*, about the bond between an 'orphaned' boy and a horse) who wrote the screenplay. Top independent filmmaker John Sayles had written a script for Spielberg called *Night Skies* about an alien stranded on earth, though it was not developed further. Legendary *Star Wars* concept illustrator Ralph McQuarrie designed ET's ship and Industrial Light And Magic provided visual effects, under the direction of Dennis Muren who began his collaboration with Spielberg on this film. When the film was released in summer 1982 *ET* became a worldwide phenomenon, unsurprisingly seen as symbolic of every religious icon in its representation of compassion and humility. Children even wrote letters to ET. Spielberg held out for many years before releasing the film on video, finally doing so in 1989. He has vowed to never make a sequel.

John Williams' score quotes his theme for Yoda from the score to *The Empire Strikes Back* when ET sees the kid masked as Yoda at Halloween.

In 1985, William Kotzwinkle, who wrote the ET novel, wrote a sequel novel entitled *ET and the Book of the Green Planet*. Debra Winger supplied the voice of ET. Harrison Ford wound up on the cutting room floor as Elliot's schoolteacher. (His scenes were not reinstated in re-released and expanded version released to mark its twentieth birthday. However, a picture of him in the role can be found in *ET: From Concept to Classic*, the book published to compliment the re-release.) The closing sequence of the film was originally edited for John Williams to put his score to. However, when Spielberg realised that Williams had more music to play, Spielberg told Williams to just play it and then re-edited the images to fit the music.

Verdict: One of Spielberg's iconic films, distilling all his essential themes for the first time. The film that made the director a household name. Some might say that the sentimentality displayed here negatively influenced subsequent films. Some see *ET* as the start of the director's creative decline up until *Schindler's List*. 5/5

Always (1989)

Cast: Richard Dreyfuss (Pete Sandich), Holly Hunter (Dorinda Durston), Brad Johnson (Ted Baker), John Goodman (Al Yackey), Audrey Hepburn (Hap), Roberts Blossom (Dave), Keith David (Powerhouse), Marg Helgenberger (Rachel), Dale Dye (Fire Boss), Doug McGrath (Bus Driver)

Crew: Director: Steven Spielberg, Producers: Kathleen Kennedy, Frank Marshall, Steven Spielberg, Screenplay: Jerry Belson, Based on the screenplay for *A Guy Named Joe* by Dalton Trumbo, Cinematographer: Mikael Salomon, Music :John Williams, Production Designer: James D Bissell, Editor: Michael Kahn, Visual Effects: Joe Johnston, Industrial Light and Magic, 106 minutes

Story: Pete Sandich is a fire-fighting pilot working in Montana putting out forest fires. Dorinda is his partner – working in the control tower. Their relationship is tender and deeply felt but fraught with a tension born from Pete's selfish and self-consciously daredevil attitude.

Dorinda is finding it increasingly difficult to handle the situation and she convinces him to take a safer job training other pilots. Pete's singular problem is a failure to tell Dorinda he loves her. Comic complications ensue initially when a new trainee pilot Ted Baker arrives. Soon after, Dorinda's life is shattered when Pete's plane catches fire and he dies. Pete finds himself strolling through a burnt-out forest where he meets Hap, an angel who informs Pete that he must return to the world of the living. Pete does so. Dorinda has become very withdrawn and has moved away to San Diego. Al Yackey, big-hearted mutual friend of Pete and Dorinda, has become a pilot trainer and after an argument with Dorinda, castigating her for stopping living her life, she returns to Flat Rock with him. Her friendship with rookie firefighter pilot Ted Baker develops much to Pete's jealousy and anxiety. Pete of course, cannot communicate with Dorinda and his mission is to help Ted become the best pilot he can. Sure enough, Pete overcomes his jealousy and helps Ted achieve his potential once he realises that he can communicate with him. The story culminates with a huge forest fire. Dorinda pilots a plane herself, rather than Ted Baker, against the wishes of her colleagues and friends, and in a near-death situation receives guidance from Pete, who is finally able to communicate with Dorinda. Returning safely to the ground, Dorinda walks towards her new life with Ted, Pete is at last able to let go as he strolls off towards his new life.

Themes: Learning to let go of a relationship and over-come jealousy. The need and power of inspiration, often with fear as its starting point.

The unseen guiding hand of compassion and encour-agement, in a sense an angelic, supernatural presence which is also part of the narratives of *ET*, the end of *Indiana Jones and the Last Crusade*, aspects of *Empire of the Sun* and *The Color Purple*, *Amistad* and certainly *Saving Private Ryan* with its explicit dialogue reference to angels. Early on in *Always*, Dorinda refers to Pete as Peter St Peter. The film is an easygoing celebration and affirmation of friendship and community. There are no villains in the film just a very human situation touched by tragedy and fantasy. A plane in the film has 'A Wing' and 'A Prayer' painted on its wings. Failure to communicate as source of problems – in *Always* the terrific scene when Dorinda cycles out onto the runway as Pete's plane rolls along, to tell Pete she loves him, and he does not hear because of the roar of plane engines. Minutes later he is dead. The film centres on fear of failure, fear of loneliness and fear of rejection. The film also uses flying as a narrative device but also again symbolic, particularly at the end of the story when Dorinda's plane seems to break beyond the skies and fly amongst the stars. Dorinda, early in the film, states emphatically to Peter: 'Kiss me and fly!'

As with so many other Spielberg male protagonists Pete is yet another Peter Pan figure not quite able to grow up, living in a cocoon of work and selfishness. By the end of the story Peter has moved to a more selfless level. The scene with Dorinda crying in the bedroom as Al tries to talk to her is some of the most emotionally honest and realistic scenes in all of Spielberg's movies – the bare, grey walls of Dorinda's apartment reflects her dead state of mind, contrasting with the warm cabin-like design of her home at the start of the film. The plane is used as a magical craft –the shot where Pete and Dorinda take a walk through the forest at night and see the plane, its lights on, evokes memories of ET's ship with its points of magic light amongst the fir trees. The film unsurprisingly asserts the positive power of love, both compassionate and passionate, to heal and encourage people in their daily lives. *Always* might be Spielberg's most obviously spiritual film, particularly with the images of water and fire both suggesting baptism. Dorinda flies through the flames, then crashes into the lake and resurfaces with Pete at her side.

The film is not set in a particularly recognisable environment (or one that is that common) but the emotions that play out are – the typical Spielberg formula. Once again, Spielberg creates a very specific, allegorical fantasy environment, another of his neverlands, where the drama plays out. At the close of the film the characters somehow depart for a return to real life, a return home to where they are loved and where they belong. The role of music as a connecting force – *in Close Encounters* we see it, in *Jaws* when the guys sing, in *The Color Purple*, in *Schindler's List*, in *Hook*. Pete cocky – basically still a boy. He has to mature. Dorinda is another of Spielberg's strong willed female leads who initially and jokingly refers to the dress Peter has bought her as 'girl clothes' only for one of the pilots to then tell her 'You look like an angel.' Pete neurosis fuels the pain of his return as a ghost; the bravura and joking around that he relied upon so much when he was alive are not enough to prevent the heartache he experiences watching Dorinda build a new life in his absence. *Always*, like *ET* and *The Color Purple* especially, shows that romantic love and the love of friendships can exist beyond any boundary. *Always* contains many moments of genuine everyday emotion, notably when Al and Dorinda embrace and laugh as they dance. Of Pete, Al says: 'I miss him too. I loved him like I never loved a guy. And I don't love guys.' Al is the best friend – life loving, upbeat, rather like Sallah to Indy. He is the voice of reason in the way Itzhak Stern is in *Schindler's List*.

Always focuses on ideas that had appeared in all of Spielberg's films to date and there is a very appealing melancholy about the film, such as in the moment when Pete first feels Dorinda as she touches down on her return from San Diego.

Sound and Vision Keys: Silhouette – Dorinda alone in her house in profile – her emptiness, shadow state. Slapstick humour – sight gags – very old-fashioned humour from Spielberg. Communication as salvation – express your feelings. Dorinda is rather like Tinkerbell (in *Hook*, the film, made after *Always*) when she puts her dress on. Spielberg's supernatural blue light – notice when Pete opens the fridge door, the glow of blue light across his face makes him look almost unworldly – a precursor of things to come. The blue light also becomes evident at the end of the story as Pete talks to Dorinda – his face is blue, hers has a warmer light on it.

Background: Spielberg had admired Victor Fleming's original movie *A Guy Named Joe* all his life and as far back as *Jaws* had talked with Dreyfuss about one day making the film, Dreyfuss saying that he had to appear in the eventual remake. At one point Robert Redford and Paul Newman were considered. Spielberg just kept developing it, acknowledging that he was not mature enough until the late 1980s to make it.

Visual effects involved some of the best-designed miniature model and fire effects ever seen. The special-effects unit created fake forests and hillsides inside a huge warehouse with model planes suspended from a track above. The rear projection for the close-up flight scenes of Pete, Dorinda and Al in their cockpits is exceptional. Sean Connery was originally considered for the role of Hap. Hap was Audrey Hepburn's final feature-film appearance.

Verdict: Woefully underrated. One of Spielberg's best works – perhaps it is just too whimsical. Deeply felt and very emotionally satisfying. It is not the kind of epic fantasy and adventure that Spielberg had become known for but much more a fantasy set in people's living rooms. 4/5

Hook (1991)

Cast: Robin Williams (Peter Banning/Peter Pan), Dustin Hoffman (Captain Hook), Julia Roberts (Tinkerbell), Bob Hoskins (Smee), Caroline Goodall (Moira), Maggie Smith (Wendy), Charlie Korsmo (Jack), Amber Scott (Maggie), Arthur Malet (Tootles), Dante Basco (Rufio), Glenn Close, David Crosby (Pirates)

Crew: Director: Steven Spielberg, Producers: Dodi Fayed, Craig Baumgarten, Gerald R Molen, Screenplay: Nick Castle, James V Hart, Production Designer: Norman Garwood, Visual Consultant: John Napier, Editor: Michael Kahn, Music: John Williams, Visual Effects: Industrial Light and Magic, 144 minutes

Story: Peter Pan is a ruthless 1990s lawyer named Peter Banning. When his children are kidnapped by Captain Hook, Banning is compelled to return to Neverland and begin his journey of the heart to reclaim the memory of his childhood self – Peter Pan – and to secure the safety of his family. With the encouragement of Tinkerbell, Peter enlists the help of the Lost Boys who prepare him physically and spiritually for the challenge of confronting Hook and rescuing his children. As Peter struggles to regain his old stature, Hook weasels his way into the affections of Peter's son, playing on the boy's disaffection with his father. At the last minute Peter's fate changes when he reconnects with his past in a gentle and touching recollection of his origins. Finally reconciled with his past, Peter flies again – literally and emotionally. He shares his delight with Tinkerbell who also grows up. Peter must chose between his childhood love for her and his love for his family. With his emotional tangle unravelled Peter goes forward to draw his regressive/progressive adventure to a close in a showdown with Captain Hook. Hook is defeated, his vanity and refusal to accept that time moves on proving his real downfall as he cries out for his mother. Peter says farewell to The Lost Boys and returns to his real life, reunited with his children and his wife.

Themes: Don't forget where you come from. *Hook* is Spielberg's Christmas movie and rather nicely its theme echoes one of the main ideas of *A Christmas Carol*. *Hook* also emphatically states the following: that play is good; all the world is a stage; fantasy and art have their place in helping us understand our own real-world emotional dilemmas.

The battle at the end of the movie sees childlike invention and imagination take flight and triumph over regimented adulthood – represented by Hook and his pirate militia. The film suggests the benefit of recognising that time moves on and to make the most of this fact – to 'seize the day' as Tootles exclaims – rather than deny old age as Captain Hook seems to want to. Peter must choose between his special affection for Tinkerbell and his sexual, grown-up love for his wife. Witness the scene when Peter kisses Tinkerbell. Regression can sometimes mean progression– the childish food fight and ridiculous retraining that Peter undergoes allow him to reawaken to his potential and true self. The film suggests the value of personal belief in overcoming one's fears. *Hook* clearly expresses the Spielberg idea of anxious, regressive men coming to face the real world without the protection of their own Neverland – in this case, very literally. At the start of the film, Jack Banning makes a comment to his father, Peter, about his being afraid of being sucked out of the plane (sucked out of the plane into real, messy life). The key sequence of the film is when Peter and Tinkerbell remember how they met and how Peter fell in love and grew up, culminating in the flight from The Nevertree. 'He rescued the memory of himself as a child and carried that best friend with him the rest of his life. It will never leave him again.' (Steven Spielberg in Premiere, December 1991)

Sound and Vision Keys: The teddy bear, the thimble, the cock crowing when Peter slashes the coconut to announce the dawn of his new persona, clocks, reflections. Dressing up/performance – Hook's red carpet on the ship's steps, Peter dressing up as a pirate, Peter imagining himself as Pan in order to be Pan. Storytelling – Grandma Wendy with Maggie in the tent in the bedroom, Peter giving his speech, the school play, Maggie singing, Peter and Tinkerbell recalling Peter's past in order to save him. The entire film was intentionally conceived to resemble a hybrid of film and theatre.

Background: *Hook* encapsulates many fundamental Spielbergian motifs and themes. Since the mid-1980s Spielberg had spoken of a new screen adaptation of JM Barrie's tale. At one point Spielberg was to have made the project as a musical (see Spielberg's liner notes on the soundtrack). At another time Michael Jackson was potentially to have appeared as Peter. When the film was released in 1991, many critics felt Spielberg had perhaps grown bored of the Pan concept and that the film seemed tired, over the top and lacking in any of the charm of its source material. Spielberg almost directed the remake of *Cape Fear* but instead chose to go with *Hook* – both movies came out within a month or so of one another in autumn 1991. If you think about it, *Hook* and *Cape Fear* tell pretty similar stories about an apparently happy family terrorised by a malevolent stranger who disrupts their lives and threatens to destroy the family unit forever. *Hook* was a flagship project for the new Sony Pictures studio – the film ran several months over schedule and over budget. It was shot on the same soundstages as *The Wizard of Oz*.

When Peter is taken to Neverland the couple sprinkled with fairy dust as they kiss on the bridge are George Lucas and Carrie Fisher. Michael Jackson and Quincy Jones were apparently filmed as pirates but not included in the final cut. Tinkerbell was almost portrayed by Michelle Pfeiffer. Gwyneth Paltrow appears as young Wendy in a flash-back sequence.

Verdict: An underrated Spielberg film which fell foul of its own hype – people allowed the expectation to obstruct their appreciation. Perhaps many expected a more action-orientated story – a kind of Peter Pan meets Indiana Jones. Instead, what they got was effectively a musical without songs. The film does drag slightly once Peter meets the Lost Boys. The film is alternately manic and tender. As with *Close Encounters of the Third Kind* and *Indiana Jones and the Last Crusade*, Spielberg took a very tall story and filled it with recognisable emotional confusions, especially around the relationship between fathers and sons. 3/5

From Sugarland To Omaha Beach

The Sugarland Express (1974)

Cast: Goldie Hawn (Lou Jean Poplin), Ben Johnson (Captain Tanner), Michael Sacks (Maxwell Slide), William Atherton (Clovis Poplin), Gregory Walcott (Mashburn), Steve Kanaly (Jessup), Louise Latham (Mrs Looby), Harrison Zanuck (Baby Langston), AL Camp (Mr Nocker), Jessie Lee Fulton (Mrs Nocker), Dean Smith (Russ Berry), Ted Grossman (Dietz)

Crew: Director: Steven Spielberg, Producers: David Brown, Richard Zanuck, Screenplay: Hal Barwood, Matthew Robbins, Cinematographer: Vilmos Zsigmond, Editors: Edward M Abroms, Verna Fields, Music: John Williams, 110 minutes

Story: A correctional facility in Texas – the late 1960s or early 1970s. Lou Jean Poplin arrives at the centre apparently to pay a routine visit to her husband Clovis, just four months from regaining his freedom. The charismatic Lou Jean convinces Clovis to escape and join her in a trek to get their young son, baby Langston, from the foster parents he has been placed with by the authorities. Dressing

Clovis in a plaid shirt, jeans and shades Lou Jean leads her husband to freedom and very swiftly they are en route across Sugarland, Texas. Sure enough the police are quickly alerted. Clovis and Lou Jean take a policeman, Officer Maxwell Slide, a new recruit, hostage, and use his car to get across the state. Soon, what seems to be the entire Texas police force are on their tail (like an express train) as are the media and a posse of crazed vigilantes. The police effort is led by steady and patient Captain Tanner who, despite his best efforts, can only watch helplessly as events culminate in the death of Clovis and Lou Jean.

Themes: The dominant theme at work in *Sugarland* is that of the adult as child – a concept which Spielberg would use throughout this career. Clovis and Lou Jean are both twenty-five years old going on fifteen.

Where Lou Jean is hot-headed and treats the quest as something of a game for almost its entirety, Clovis is in a state of perpetual anxiety about his predicament. As the story hurtles forward, both Lou Jean and Clovis reveal themselves to be equally fragile and equally strong, though it is Lou Jean who is the more decisive – the first of many strong Spielberg women characters. Witness Lou Jean upon arrival at the correctional facility walking confidently yet waif-like towards freeing her husband. When we first see Clovis, though, (in his all-white outfit) he walks boyishly, almost pathetically. When Clovis expresses reluctance at leaving with Lou Jean she reprimands him saying, 'Clovis Poplin have you forgotten your own son?' This issue of memory and recalling family bonds will reverberate from hereon throughout Spielberg's films as a director. Lou Jean's determined love for her son pre-empts that of Jillian Guiler's for Barry in *Close Encounters*. There is a facial similarity between Lou Jean and Jillian. Lou Jean has a rescue mission to accomplish – the first of many in Spielberg's films and undoubtedly this entry has the bleakest outcome. Clovis and Lou Jean become fugitive children. These lovers on the run are just kids struggling to find a place in the real, adult world, echoing the protagonists in Nicholas Ray's *They Live By Night* and those in Terrence Malick's *Badlands*. Captain Tanner describes Clovis and Lou Jean as '. . . nothing but a couple of kids.' This is an observation born out most obviously in a moment of vintage Spielberg solace when Clovis and Lou Jean, holed up in a camper van, watch a Road Runner cartoon adding their own sound effects. 'If baby Langston were here we'd be a real family,' Lou Jean states emphatically. Like children, both Clovis and Lou Jean are anxious about their ability to parent and their ability to survive the ordeal they have created for themselves. Lou Jean frets, saying: 'What they [the authorities and media] are saying is I'm an unfit mother.' Like all children, Lou Jean and especially Clovis need to trust an authority figure, a parent if you like, and in this film that is Captain Tanner. Tanner is the first in a long line of protective father figures which will include Keys, John Quincy Adams, Oskar Schindler, Captain John Miller and even Indiana Jones. Through the film, Tanner and Clovis talk over the car radios and Tanner asks Clovis, 'Do you trust me?' The Captain empathises and the unexpected bond between him and the Poplins is brilliantly and economically expressed when Spielberg unites the three of them in one image. In the top part of the frame we see Tanner's eyes reflected in his rear-view mirror and in the bottom of the frame we see Clovis and Lou Jean looking at him from the back seat of the car in front of Tanner's.

Clovis and Lou Jean are not the only children in the film. The third is Officer Maxwell Slide. Looking similar to Clovis, though having softer features, Slide is like the other half of Clovis – they are both roughly the same age. *The Sugarland Express* even ends on an image of Tanner and Slide standing together, silhouetted against golden sunlight on a river.

The Sugarland Express is packed with the germs of many recurring Spielberg ideas and themes. For all Spielberg's affinity for fantasy environments in his subsequent films, *The Sugarland Express* reveals his acute sense of place and his ability to capture local colour. Look at the first image in the film – a long lonesome highway and a dizzying array of radio signs, more confusing than clear. It is against this that we first meet Lou Jean – it is no wonder that she will feel helpless and lacking in direction.

Spielberg's liberal sensibilities also shine through in this film, particularly its commentary on vigilante culture and also through the empathy Tanner displays for the criminals. He is on the side of the kids just as Keys is in *ET: The Extra Terrestrial* and as John Quincy Adams is on the side of Cinque and Baldwin in *Amistad*. In this film, the police become a menacing presence as they rise up from the highway rather like a shark will arise from the waters in Spielberg's following film, also produced by Zanuck/ Brown. In *ET*, the threat of police/authority is very evident (in this film and in ET the authorities invade the home) and propels the film's subplot and its thrilling and jubilant climactic chase.

Family counts the most – whether biological or social. Lou Jean and Clovis love their son so much they risk death itself. Inside the car with Officer Slide they create another family unit with Lou Jean the more proactive, strong figure. Strong mother figures and the often weak and confused men are Spielberg characters and the desire to create and maintain a family is a Spielberg theme.

Sound and Vision Keys: The characters make a journey of emotion and geography and Spielberg signals this sense of movement and kinetic energy through wide shots of roads and frequent inclusion of road signs in the frame. Whilst filmed in an essentially naturalistic way (the film is based on real events) Spielberg and Vilmos Zsigmond also lend the film a quirkier, somewhat cartoonish quality – for example the rotating chicken sign, the long trail of cars. The humour of Chuck Jones' cartoons has certainly influenced Spielberg's visual humour.

Spielberg shoots with a long lens, compressing distance and lending much of the narrative a documentary, vérité feel – a technique enhanced by much of the film being shot hand-held inside the car that Lou Jean and Clovis have hijacked. It would not be until *Schindler's List* and *Saving Private Ryan* that he would return to this kind of approach. Spielberg also begins to employ his trademark facility with more sweeping compositions as he frames the Texas landscape. There is a bleakness to the story – which returns in moments in some of the later films, notably *Empire of the Sun* and *Saving Private Ryan*. Spielberg's visual presentation of the startlingly fastidious, cold middle-class foster parents contrasts with Clovis and Lou Jean's crumpled charm.

As in so many other Spielberg films, reflections are used to enhance the drama and compress ideas – the reflection of the Road Runner cartoon in the window of the camper van as Lou Jean and Clovis look naively out of it. In other films Spielberg uses cartoon footage to emphasise a dramatic moment, a turning point. The sunset at the end of the film brings a natural, inevitable end to the story and is the first of many sunsets in his films, announcing a comforting sense of closure and usually reconciliation. John Williams' score for *The Sugarland Express* was his first collaboration with Steven Spielberg. Spielberg had initially hoped for something grandly American, rather like Aaron Copland's brilliant *Appalachian Spring*. Instead, and true to form, Williams created something a little more unique but still utterly American – small-scale theme led by harmonica. It is a theme which emphasises not the chase aspect of the story but the wistful, childlike aspect of the characters. Occasionally a martial theme is introduced and only once does anything approaching eerie dissonance sound out, during the edgy shoot-out scene.

Background: *The Sugarland Express* was Spielberg's first theatrical feature. He discovered the story in a newspaper and worked it up into a film story with Matthew Robbins and Hal Barwood, both of whom play the Navy pilots who emerge from the Mothership in *Close Encounters*. Robbins went on to direct **batteries not included* for Spielberg's Amblin Entertainment. The film was released and failed to impact commercially, perhaps because of its downbeat ending, but perhaps also because lovers-on-the-run films had become a popular subgenre at the time, notably with the very different *Badlands* and *Thieves Like Us*. In 1993 a film was released called *A Perfect World*, directed by Clint Eastwood. Spielberg had considered directing it – not difficult to understand given the story's father/son dynamic.

Verdict: Fascinating but not only because it is Spielberg's first feature. A well-crafted film some may wish had marked the kinds of films Spielberg would go on to direct. Hopefully he will one day tell another story of working-class Americans. 4/5

Close Encounters of the Third Kind (1977)

Cast: Richard Dreyfuss (Roy Neary), Melinda Dillon (Jillian Guiler), Terri Garr (Ronnie), Cary Guffey (Barry Guiler), Bob Balaban (David Laughlin), François Truffaut (Claude Lacombe), J Patrick McNamara (Project Leader), Warren J Kemmering (Wild Bill), Roberts Blossom (Farmer), Philip Dodds (Jean Claude), Shawn Bishop (Neary Child), Adrienne Campbell (Neary Child), Justin Dreyfuss (Toby Neary), Lance Henriksen (Robert), Merrill Connally (Team Leader), George DiCenzo (Major Benchley)

Crew: Director: Steven Spielberg, Producers; Julia Phillips, Michael Phillips, Screenplay: Steven Spielberg, Cinematographer: Vilmos Zsigmond, Production

Designer: Joe Alves, Editor: Michael Kahn, Music: John Williams, Special Visual Effects: Douglas Trumbull, 135 minutes, (132 minutes, Special Edition, released in 1980)

Story: The Sonora Desert, 1977. A scientific research team discover several World War II bomber planes marooned in the desert – the very planes that were recorded missing during the war. There is no apparent explanation other than the poetic, prophetic ramblings of a local desert man who, as he is translated, says that 'last night the sun came up and sang to him.'

Muncie, Indiana. Single mother Jillian Guiler lives with her son Barry. Unable to sleep, Barry is awoken by his toys as they magically come to life. White lights sweep silently and menacingly across the wall of his room. Barry rushes out into the starry night to investigate. In a suburban home, the Neary family, headed by Roy and Ronnie, go about a typical evening. Roy, an electrical engineer, is called out to see to a power cut which has wiped out an entire town's supply. As Roy races to deal with the problem, he witnesses a bright light which blasts down on him from the night sky above. It is his moment of transformation and his life will never be the same. He races to pursue the light in the sky as they dart along like sky pixies. Roy slams to a halt almost knocking over Barry Guiler as his mother rushes to pick him up. Roy and Jillian introduce themselves to one another then discover they are in the presence of skywatchers. Charged with a renewed passion, Roy obsesses about the UFOs and his family life fractures as his obsession strengthens. At her farmhouse, Jillian is revisited by the UFOs and this time

Barry goes to the light and is 'abducted' by the unseen, unknowable force. Anticipating the arrival of the UFOs, scientists and military intelligence secure the area around Devil's Tower in Wyoming, creating a fake anthrax scare as masses of local people are ferried out by the government on trains (in scenes that predate *Schindler's List*). With Roy's marriage in tatters he teams up with Jillian and together they crack the code of where the aliens will arrive and travel to Devil's Tower. The film's final movement finds Roy and Jillian overlooking the airstrip where the aliens will hopefully land. They arrive and Jillian is reunited with her son. Roy goes aboard the Mothership and it lifts into the stars.

Themes: *Close Encounters* is proof of Spielberg's affection for the road movie format; here, and time and again in later works, the literal journey across a landscape also expresses the emotional odyssey being undertaken by the protagonist. Perhaps Spielberg's greatest accomplishment in this film is not in its integration of effects or its scale and narrative pull but in the human-scale drama that plays out around Roy Neary and his lower middle-class lifestyle. In the original edition, Roy's breakdown and manic behaviour achieve almost comic proportions, threatening to lessen our sympathy for his confusion and discovery of a new meaning in his life. Spielberg galvanises his sympathy for the middle-class American psyche – this is a movie about many of the people in his audience.

Neary's story is the story of a man pursuing a dream with risks to the emotional stability of his family. Early in the tale he loses his job, thereby freeing him up to the greater, more spiritual adventure (along with *ET*, *Always* and *Empire Of the Sun* it is one of Spielberg's more overtly spiritual films). Roy Neary is one of Spielberg's most obvious Peter Pan/Manchild figures who selfishly leaves his family to satisfy his own emotional needs. Twenty years after the film was made, Spielberg, in a short documentary (*Close Encounters: A Look Back*) by Laurent Bouzereau, stated that had he made the film in the 1990s Roy Neary would not have given up on his family. Jillian is the typically strong and resourceful mother figure. Roy and Jillian join together to retrieve a lost child (evoking Clovis and Lou Jean, Captain Miller searching for Private Ryan or Peter Banning going to rescue his children) held by a force larger than either of them. In this film, Spielberg announces what would be an ever-intensifying affirmation of the place of the unseen and unknowable as a force for good. Neary's life is injected with a fresh sense of purpose and could be said to become more authentic as he undertakes his mission (rather like Henry Jones senior breaking out of academic thought into a world of action in *Indiana Jones and the Last Crusade*) risking his sanity, the world he knows, his safety – he sacrifices everything to secure his mission. The film's reference ton Pinocchio indicates Neary has a wish (upon a star – almost literally) and he embarks on fulfilling that wish. With *AI* (2001), Spielberg returned to the Pinocchio motif in the story of a boy robot who seeks more human engagement. Roy Neary too sought a means to reawaken him to being alive, to feeling human. *Close Encounters* testifies to Spielberg's ongoing scepticism about authority – the villain of the piece is the machinery of government which is shown as invasive and devious as in *ET* and *The Sugarland Express*.

In *Close Encounters*, Spielberg's plucky, little guy heroes find a way to subvert authority and make the most meaningful contact with the extraterrestrials, who embody the spirit of communication and also playfulness. Lacombe, a precursor to Keys (with Roy as Elliot) is the only authority figure in the film who is really able to connect with the aliens, and in a sense with the openness of childhood, through his hand signals. Words are not enough. *Close Encounters* celebrates the non-verbal as a key to connection. This idea repeats through numerous Spielberg films – ET's finger to Elliot's forehead, Henry Jones' embrace of his son Indiana, ghost-Pete dancing with Dorinda, Cinque and Roger clutching hands at the end of the trial.

Sound and Vision Keys: The Spielberg motif of illumination is overtly played out through this film – Barry Guiler opens the kitchen door only to be blasted with intense bright light. Roy Neary at the end of the film enters into the light emanating from the Mothership – his own process of illumination complete and also just beginning by his decision to break away from the confines of his safe and familiar world. Spielberg tracks toward the action to intensify our sense of urgency –such as when the planes are discovered at the start of the film. Again, Spielberg displays his skill in eliciting strong performances from children.

The film contains some of Spielberg's most honest direction of his actors – witness the scene when Roy is found by Ronnie in the shower fully-clothed – a break-down not repeated in its frailty until Dorinda's grieving in *Always* and Captain Miller's sobbing in *Saving Private Ryan*.

Close Encounters announces Spielberg's fascination with World War II. The film works because of its rooting in reality. Mystery can give way to wonder and also a little fear as in the Mongolia sequence when the scientists are led to a huge tanker marooned in the sand.

Spielberg ably emphasises menace through suggestion as in the besieged kitchen sequence – watch the screws rotating out of their sockets in the grille. A sinister humour is at work too, notably in the playful, somehow alive, toys. It is as though the whole world, particularly the known, is not that far removed from some other version of itself.

In *Close Encounters*, as in many of Spielberg's later films, the child is the wisest character – the one most attuned to the incredible events unfolding. Barry Guiler is the character who first connects with the visitors and who also displays no fear of them; witness his smile to some unseen presence when the extraterrestrials arrive. *ET* clearly develops this theme of the positive openness of children. This openness to difference is shown as a source of salvation, especially for Roy and Jillian whose relationship blossoms. Their intense hug at the railway station is echoed by Alan and Ellie's embrace at a critical moment in *Jurassic Park*.

Background: *After Close Encounters of the Third Kind, AI* is the only feature that Spielberg has written and directed. *Close Encounters* is a development of his amateur movie,

Firelight. Testifying to Spielberg's respect for the place of music in his films, John Williams came on board the project before it was completed. Released just six months after *Star Wars* (1977 was some year at the movies), *Close Encounters* was, apart from its spectacle, the antithesis of *Star Wars*. Spielberg originally had Paul Schrader write a screenplay based on Spielberg's central concept. However, Schrader's script centred on a military intelligence man. Spielberg wanted someone who ate at McDonald's.

The ominous cloud effects were created by inverting the camera and filming paint being poured into a tank of water. Two concepts that never made the final cut were flying extraterrestrials at the end of the movie and also lots of brightly shining flying cubes that preceded the arrival of the big ships. Actress Melinda Dillon was not told that the kitchen would erupt around her in the scene where the aliens invade and take Barry. Child actor Cary Guffey did not know what was going to happen. Jillian's shocked screams are for real. In 1980, Spielberg released a Special Edition which revealed the interior of the Mothership with Neary walking around inside it. Spielberg also contracted the centre movement of the film, abbreviating the government cover-up and Neary's breakdown.

Verdict: *Close Encounters* is perhaps still the ultimate Spielberg film, with its integration of small-scale human drama set against a spectacular canvas in which characters must group together to survive chaos. It was the first time Spielberg really drew together the key themes he would revisit all through his career to follow in its celebration of peace, love, community, the fulfilment of a wish and communication. The film also offers us one of Richard Dreyfuss' best performances – anxious, hopeful, funny, energetic, sympathetic. 5/5

1941 (1979)

Cast: Dan Aykroyd (Sergeant Tree), Ned Beatty (Ward Douglas), John Belushi (Wild Bill Kelso), Lorraine Gary (Joan Douglas), Murray Hamilton (Claude), Christopher Lee (Von Kleinschmidt), Tim Matheson (Birkhead), Toshiro Mifune (Commander Mitamura), Warren Oates (Maddox), Robert Stack (General Stilwell), Treat Williams (Starski), Nancy Allen (Donna), John Candy (Foley), Eddie Deezen (Herbie), Bobby Di Cicco (Wally), Slim Pickens (Hollis Wood), Wendie Jo Sperber (Maxine), Lionel Stander (Scioli)

Crew: Director: Steven Spielberg, Producers: Buzz Feitshans, Janet Healey (Associate Producer), Michael Kahn (Associate Producer), John Milius (Executive Producer), Writers: Robert Zemeckis, Bob Gale, Cinematographer: William A Fraker, Production Designer: Dean Edward Mitzner, Editor: Michael Kahn, Music: John Williams, Special Visual Effects: Greg Jein, 118 minutes

Story: December 13 1941. A Japanese submarine emerges (with visually amusing results) off the West Coast of America just one week after the bombing of Pearl Harbour. Soon enough the population of Los Angeles is alerted to the potential threat and so begins a frantic, crazed, gargantually chaotic effort by the military and the

American public to protect their country from attack. The film's narrative follows the bungled, botched and brave efforts of many characters: the young American soldiers who commandeer a tank through the streets of LA; the off-course Wild Bill Kelso, lost en route to LA from San Francisco in his fighter plane; General Stillwell's efforts to maintain order on the streets and amongst his troops; the Douglas family as they defend their cliff-top home from the sub; Hollis P Wood and his face-to-face encounter with the Japanese sub crew; the efforts of Sikarski to gain the attentions of Betty Douglas in the process vying with Wally – their competitiveness coming to a head in a USO dance; crazed Colonel Maddox out in the desert waiting to fend off attacking Japanese; George and his son on the Ferris wheel, armed and on the lookout; Loomis and Donna's efforts to have sex in a plane whilst airborne. The film rotates amongst these frantic storylines and culminates with the troops launching fire at the sub and with Wild Bill swimming aboard the sub. It concludes with the sun rising over an unthreatened Los Angeles and one last immense sight gag – his house already ravaged by tanks and machine-gun fire, Mr Douglas nails the advent wreath onto the front door. This is the last straw and the house just falls away and over the cliff top.

Themes: Perhaps Spielberg's most notorious film – a massive visual joke which, as the final credits roll, you cannot help laughing with: all that effort and energy expended on such a small idea. The film starts at a comic fever pitch and continues, never allowing the audience a quiet moment. This blind faith in such hyperkinetic, loud comedy is appealing. The film is a series of huge and brilliantly staged sight gags. And that's all.

In a very simplistic way, the film presents a familiar Spielberg premise – a family and community under threat from an outside force beyond their comprehension. Several of the characters are recognisably Spielbergian in their design. Wally, particularly, is another Spielberg Manchild. He wants to get into the army but at the same time he has a gentility and grace which is mocked by the comically gruff soldiers he encounters. Nonetheless, in Spielberg's filmic world it is Wally and not the gruff slick Sikarski who emerges victorious. Wally even dons a soldier's uniform towards the end of the film, is mistaken for a Sergeant and leads the other soldiers into action. As such Wally is not a million miles from Peter Banning. In a terrific two-part essay in the magazine

Film Comment, writer Henry Sheehan traces the Lost Boy-Peter Pan theme through every Spielberg film and remarkably 1941 does present this central preoccupation with real clarity. In this film most of the characters are lost. It is only General Stillwell (his name carrying the meaning of his character) who registers any kind of calm – another father figure presiding over the chaos. Stillwell's big quirk, as Henry Sheehan noted in his essay, is his determination to see Dumbo play at the cinema. Stillwell is able to shed a tear and get completely engrossed. It somehow seems to steady him and allows him to return back to work with a sure sense of purpose. Wally is the only character close to Stillwell –neither man has that gruff, macho attitude which throughout the film Spielberg lampoons.

The Douglas family is the typical Spielberg family yet

they do not get sufficient screen time to make us empathise with them in any real way. There is a glimmer of the strong Spielberg mother figure who says to her husband: 'I refuse to let you bring the war into my own front yard.' Instead we return to the house only to see it in an ever increasing state of destruction.

It would be wrong to watch *1941* as an approximation of the American home front effort. Spielberg has told how John Wayne apparently hated the film for its depiction of buffoon-ish Americans and had even encouraged Spielberg not to make it. Conversely, you could say the film celebrates a down-home heroism – witness Hollis P Wood's childish, playful (and far from threatening) escape from the submarine. The film has a vulgar streak and is essentially very juvenile delighting in images of fighter planes pulling up at gas stations for refills. Wild Bill is as anxious about achieving his mission as, for example, Clovis is of finding baby Langston in *The Sugarland Express* or Peter Banning is of rescuing his kids and getting back home. In *1941* the faces of authority and government are the most inept and it is the common man who makes the bravest and admirable effort.

Sound and Vision Keys: Spielberg plays on our fascination with scale, physical chaos and destruction. Everything is subservient to collisions, explosions and intrusions. Perhaps the classic Spielberg shot in the film is early on when Donna approaches the American bomber, the camera low to the ground, tracking in behind her towards the plane whilst John Williams' score plays it straight. It is a shot which predates the kind of shots venerating planes that we see in *Empire of the Sun* and *Always* (which occasionally revels in slapstick), *1941* makes obvious. Spielberg's affinity for slapstick humour, though it is fair to say that his experience on *1941* made him reluctant about making another comedy; dramas with comic moments fine but not all-out comedy.

Background: Originally titled *The Night the Japs Attacked* and *Japs*, the screenplay was written by ace Spielberg protégés Robert Zemeckis and Bob Gale who went on to do *Back to the Future*. The script exhibits the same frantic energy that fuels all of their scripts. *1941* was a very expensive production with its huge sets and incredible miniature special-effects photography – in the digital age of today it is fascinating to watch an effects-heavy film using so many miniatures and scale models.

The woman who takes a swim in the opening of *1941* is Susan Backlinie who also took a dip at the start of *Jaws*.

Verdict: A very funny film in many places but the least thematically satisfying of all Spielberg's films, although there are glimmers of his usually more developed concerns. You have to applaud its size in pursuit of such a silly idea. 2/5

The Color Purple (1985)

Cast: Danny Glover (Albert), Whoopi Goldberg (Celie), Margaret Avery (Shug), Oprah Winfrey (Sofia), Willard E Pugh (Harpo), Akosua Busia (Nettie), Desreta Jackson (Young Celie), Adolph Caesar (Old Mr), Rae Dawn

Chong (Squeak), Dana Ivey (Miss Millie), Leonard Jackson (Pa), Bennet Guilory (Grady), John Patton Jr (Preacher), Carl Anderson (Reverend Samuel), Susan Beaubian (Corrine), James Tillis (Buster), Phillip Strong (Mayor), Laurence Fishburne (Swain), Peto Kinsaka (Adam), Lelo Masamba (Olivia), Margaret Freeman (Odessa), Howard Starr (Young Harpo), Daphaine Oliver (Young Olivia), Jadili Johnson (Young Adam), Lillian Nioki Distefano (Young Tashi)

Crew: Director: Steven Spielberg, Producers: Peter Guber (Executive Producer), Carol Isenberg (Associate Producer), Quincy Jones, Frank Marshall, Kathleen Kennedy, Steven Spielberg, Screenplay: Alice Walker, Menno Meyjes, Novel: Alice Walker, Cinematographer: Allen Daviau, Production Designer: J Michael Riva, Editor; Michael Kahn, Music: Chris Boardan, Jorge Calandrelli, Andrae Crouch, Jack Hayes, Jerry Hey, Quincy Jones, Randy Kerber, Jeremy Lubbock, Joel Rosenbaum, Caiphus Semnya, Fred Steiner, Rod Temperton, 152 minutes

Story: 1909. Young Celie Johnson gives birth to a baby girl who is taken away immediately by Celie's father – he is the father of the child. With only her sister Nettie as a source of strength Celie's life is soon ruptured again when local farmer Mr decides she will be his wife. Celie goes to live with Mr and Nettie comes to visit. Celie is living the life of a slave and has no way of expressing herself. When Nettie fights back against Mr's advances on her he orders her off his property and so begins a long period of separation between the two sisters. Celie's life becomes increasingly bleak until the arrival of Mr's lover, Shug Avery – a sassy, apparently confident jookjoint singer. She immediately takes to Celie and begins to help her find a way to express herself. Celie begins to find her voice and so starts to reclaim her identity. And as her emotional journey brightens so too does her clothing – becoming more decorative.

At her father's funeral, though dressed in black, Celie wears bright red gloves. Shug too embarks on her own emotional journey of reunion with her preacher father who objects to her lifestyle. As Celie's family and friends endure the trials of life, the narrative culminates with the discovery of letters that Nettie has written from Africa over a thirty-year period. Mr has kept them hidden from Celie all along. She discovers that her two children are still alive. The film ends with Celie being reunited with her sister and two children, Spielberg's camera perfectly capturing Celie's exhaustion in her face as she runs towards her family.

Themes: *The Color Purple* affirms faith, hope, solace, loneliness and the power of home (and its metaphorical impression). In Celie (played brilliantly by Whoopi Goldberg in her theatrical film debut) Spielberg builds a character who is effectively a sister to ET, Roy Neary and Cinque – disaffected, alone and struggling to find a way to belong and touch base with home again, whether emotionally or more physically. Celie has a dream – to see her children again – and the film charts her emotional journey to this point. She even seems to possess a magic rather like ET does. Watch how Celie wards off Mr with her hand, saying: 'Everything you done to me, I already done to you. I'm poor, black, I may even be ugly, but dear God I'm here.' The film was at one point to be called *Watch for Me in the Sunset*.

Celie's journey of illumination sees her discover her own potential and place in the world. The film's poster is built around the image of the sun – of illumination. All through the film Spielberg references the sun and uses silhouettes – witness Celie on the porch silhouetted by the setting sun or the terrific end shot where the family is reunited. Celie is aided and encouraged by a conscience figure in the character of Shug Avery – Celie's angel on her shoulder, as is Nettie through her letters. All through his career, Spielberg has placed such characters alongside his protagonists – rather in the way that Jiminy Cricket aids and encourages Pinocchio. Very early on, Celie's sister Nettie says: 'You gotta fight Celie, you got to,' to which Celie replies, 'I don't know how to fight, all I know is how to survive.' As in *Always*, *Amistad* and *ET*, love and the bonds of family and tradition exist beyond physical limits. Nettie's last words to Celie (as she is thrown off the farm by Mr) are: 'Nothing but death can keep me from here.' This sequence is one of the most openly emotional in any Spielberg film as the two sisters are violently separated by Mr. Celie and Nettie clap at one another for the last time. Celie and Nettie sign to one another one last time – their hand signals stronger than any words or opposing force, rather like those which Lacombe uses to communicate at the end of *Close Encounters*.

In Spielberg's films the hands become, obviously but

powerfully, markers of connection. *The Color Purple*, like *ET*, places a lot of dramatic emphasis on the home and the rooms and spaces of a home in a way that recalls the work of director John Ford. The film connects to *Saving Private Ryan* in its use of the porch as the place of great drama. Celie looking into the distance at the approaching car is a moment evoked very strongly at the start of *Saving Private Ryan* – we never see Mrs Ryan's distressed face, though such a shot was filmed. Spielberg uses foreground/background framing, e.g. Nettie looking through the window at Mr who is framed by the frost on the glass. Cross-cutting is used to build tension, like when Celie is going to shave Mr for the second time, intercut with African ritual, as Shug runs to stop Celie killing Mr.

The film's cinematographer, Allen Daviau (who had worked with Spielberg on the short *Amblin'*), gives the film a purple/pink tone almost throughout. The film is lit rather like *ET* at times – when Celie reads her sister's letters, a process of illumination and grace, it is as though all the positive energy of Nettie is pouring in through the window.

In *The Color Purple* play is a binding, empowering force. Recall the shadow hand-clapping of Nettie and Celie early in the film which is referenced in the moment when they are separated by Mr. Their use of hands to remain connected carries a spiritual quality which evokes the gesture of *ET* putting his finger to Elliot's head.

After *Hook* and *Empire of the Sun*, *The Color Purple* is the closest Spielberg has come to giving his narrative an outright musical moment.

In this case, Shug leads the parade from the church as

everyone sings, the camera booming up in classic Minnelli style above the action as the film musically plays out its theme of love and community.

Sound and Vision Keys: In so many of his films, rather in the spirit of animation, Spielberg anthropomorphises objects and locations – he gives them an almost human presence. In *The Color Purple* the camera tracks towards a tree/post box in such a way that makes it a character – somehow anticipating events and sometimes ominously but wisely looking on as it announces the changes and progressions in the story. Natural sunlight pouring in through a window evokes ET and represents positive emotion – recall the scene with Shug and Celie on the bed when Celie awakens to her own beauty. As in *Close Encounters of the Third Kind* the sky is the announcer of change, of the presence of something mystical – in *The Color Purple* that is Shug Avery.

The film seems to conclude that everybody belongs somewhere and that everyone can somehow go home and find love. Even Mr finds redemption in the film, in keeping somewhat with classic Hollywood drama. Shug too redeems herself through reconciliation with her disapproving preacher father. Harpo, Mr's son, also returns to his father yet their embrace is tellingly clumsy and brief. All three characters return home in some way.

As in so many melodramas, the mirror is symbolically a reflection of the soul, of a character's development. It is in her reflection that Celie, all dressed up, is finally able to laugh without raising her hand to her mouth to hide her smile. At certain points in the film Spielberg displays a very confident economy of style – such as the sequence where Celie goes from being a young teenager to a young woman.

Before we see the film's first image we hear the sounds of children's voices. Spielberg repeats this technique in many of his films: before we see the world he is taking us to, we hear it and somehow we are immersed in it more vividly. The artifice is broken down. The tracking camera, like in the rapturous opening sequence, explores the exhilaration of play and togetherness.

Spielberg uses sound to identify. For example, every time the mailman arrives we hear him first, which builds anticipation.

Background: Producer Kathleen Kennedy suggested Spielberg might be suitable for the project. Some asked if Spielberg was the right director for the job. Clearly he was because the film holds so many of the ideas and outlooks that are present through so much of his work. *The Color Purple* is the only theatrical Spielberg film to date not scored by John Williams. The film marks Oprah Winfrey's feature-film debut. (And yes, that's Laurence Fishburne as Swain.) At the time of its release the film was greeted with applause and reservation. For many the film was a successful revival of the women's picture. Eleven Oscar nominations and not one win.

Verdict: Vintage Spielberg. To date, it is still his only all-out melodrama and after *ET* his boldest statement about the power of love in all its forms and the workings of family. As Shug says, 'Everything want to be loved.' Perhaps this film truly marked his auteur status because whilst being an adaptation it absolutely bears his distinctive approach to cinema. One of the great Spielberg endings. Some of the comedy rings hollow rather in the way some of John Ford's humour did. 4/5

Empire of the Sun (1987)

Cast: Christian Bale (Jim Graham), John Malkovich (Basie), Miranda Richardson (Mrs Victor), Nigel Havers (Dr Rawlins), Joe Pantoliano (Frank Demarest), Leslie Phillips (Maxton), Masato Ibu (Sgt Nagata), Emily Richard (Jim's Mother), Rupert Frazer (Jim's Father), Peter Gale (Mr Victor), Takatoro Kataoka (Kamikaze Boy), Ben Stiller (Dainty)

Crew: Director: Steven Spielberg, Producers: Steven Spielberg, Kathleen Kennedy, Chris Kenny (Associate Producer), Frank Marshall (Executive Producer), Robert Shapiro (Executive Producer), Screenplay: Tom Stoppard, Novel: JG Ballard, Cinematographer: Allen Daviau, Production Designer: Fred Hole/Norman Reynolds, Editor: Michael Kahn, Music: John Williams, 154 minutes

Story: Shanghai, World War II. British expatriates are living comfortably in a suburbia fashioned after those of London. Jim Graham is a brash, mischievous, strong-headed boy living with his parents, attending school and singing angelically in the choir. When the Japanese invade Shanghai, Jim's secure, exotic world is smashed – he is separated from his parents. Returning home he discovers it has been ransacked by the invading forces. Suddenly, Jim hits survival mode as he eats what remains of the food in the kitchen. Returning to the city he is discovered by two American men, Basie and Frank, who feed Jim and initiate him into the darker side of life. Soon enough, the three of them are caught by the Japanese and taken to a vast holding area for new prisoners.

From here the POWs are trucked out to a remote airstrip where an expansive POW camp has been constructed. What appears to be the end of the line will be, for Jim, a vivid and illuminating journey. Jim's survivalist sense rapidly develops as he befriends over-worked Dr Rawlins and maintains his friendship with Basie in the American hut. As the trauma of living in a camp overwhelms many, Jim becomes increasingly strong, to some degree exulting in his new, strange, intense life.

Jim befriends a young Japanese boy pilot, destined for a Kamikaze run, on the other side of the fence. Gradually, Jim's manic energy and mischief become harsher and more frenzied as he witnesses death and fragility all around him. The POWs are moved out of the camp and marched across the wasteland to a huge stadium filled like an auction house with the trophies of the British homes – furniture, vehicles, and clothing. Jim continues on and witnesses the blast of the atom bomb. As he becomes increasingly frail and returns to Soochow camp, he is found by an American army unit and returned to Shanghai where he is reunited with his parents.

Themes: The character of Jim Graham is another resourceful and appealing child hero but he also has a facility for edgy, selfish, unappealing behaviour in keeping with his need to survive. From *Empire of the Sun* onwards Spielberg frequently invested his films with a certain mania and clear sense of how things can appear one way only to very quickly slide another. It is an uneasiness which finds its way appropriately into *Schindler's List*, *Amistad* and *Saving Private Ryan*. *Empire of the Sun* remains one of Spielberg's richest films, never negating his investment in spectacle and hope, instead supplementing it with a more certain sense of chaos and, most importantly, anxiety. Childhood and adulthood collide in this film.

The film is set in a location and geography away from the familiar, real world. Jim is transplanted from home to a Prisoner Of War camp where he undergoes a process of maturation and illumination. Whilst the POW camp does not perhaps appear that traumatic and is thus perhaps not historically realistic, its function in dramatic terms is to provide Jim with a playground of sorts in which to understand the world, Jim is in as much of a wilderness as Alan Grant in *Jurassic Park*, as Peter Banning is when he arrives in Neverland or when Martin Brody sets out into the sea in *Jaws*.

Jim is cared for by several parental figures. Basie is the biggest – Jim idolises him. Basie is dressed like the comic book hero on the cover of the comic Jim reads early in the film. Later in the film, Jim dresses like Basie too. In this film, adults cannot always be trusted – see how Basie just ignores Jim once on board the truck and starts talking to some new children. At the end of the film, Basie escapes (though we do not see this) and Jim's distress is strong. It anticipates the distress of the children in the car in *Jurassic Park* when Grant leaves them to fend off the T Rex.

As in so many Spielberg films the implication of an unseen presence in the lives of the protagonists is a key part of the story, though in this film the concept is given significant dialogue time throughout. Early in the film, Jim says to his mother: 'I was dreaming about God . . .. perhaps that's where God is all the time . . . perhaps he's our dream and we're his.' Interestingly, his mother is unable to answer him and shuts the door on Jim in his room. Jim asks one more question, 'If God is above us, does it mean like flying?'

Later, Jim witnesses the bomb aftershock of Hiroshima but initially believes it to be 'a white light, I thought it was Mrs Victor's soul going up to heaven.' Only when he stumbles past a radio broadcast does Jim realise he witnessed the aftershock of the atom bomb which he describes as being 'like God taking a photograph.' Jim finds a strange unexpected beauty in such horror. The food parcels dropping from the sky suggest the presence of an unseen helping hand because the scene has no visual reference to the implied aeroplane above. When Jim arrives at the POW camp he approaches a plane, putting his hand to it. As sparks fall around him, like stars, Jim is momentarily at peace – he very literally touches his dream in a moment of solace (synch sound drops out, only the music plays) away from the chaos outside. This moment recalls the silence of ET and Elliot's first encounter in Elliot's room.

The obviously spiritual aspect of Jim's character also manifests itself in what he does as much as what he says – soon after arrival at the camp, under the tutelage and protection of Dr Rawlins, Jim is asked to help out with a patient. Jim thinks he has resuscitated her. Dr Rawlins explains otherwise. Towards the end of the film, this moment is replayed with more emotion as Jim struggles to revive his dying Kamikaze pilot friend. Spielberg's camera slowly closes in on Jim's anxious face as he obsessively states: 'I can bring everyone back.' Sunlight flickers into frame as Jim rocks back and forth. The moment connects with the revival aspect of *ET* – of characters being reborn. As Jim attempts to resuscitate his friend, for an instant Jim sees himself lying on the ground in his school clothes – in effect the ghost of his former self.

As the film progresses, Jim has distinct forms of dress – his school uniform, then his Sinbad the Sailor costume. This Sinbad sequence emphasises Jim's obsession with flight and also the importance of play and solace as Spielberg invests a crashed plane with life just as Jim's imagination does. *Empire of the Sun*, like other Spielberg movies, builds its drama around the creation of new families. Dr Rawlins becomes something of a father figure to Jim, slightly resembling Jim's natural father. Basie is very much the big brother figure whose fallibility Jim begins to recognise in time. As with all Spielberg's films, the adult hero is defined by a sense of guardianship over the child who unexpectedly falls into their care. Jim is also taken care of by the ghostly Mrs Victor who, like a surrogate mother, prepares a corner of her room for him, putting up what appears to be the most important picture – Norman Rockwell's painting *Freedom From Fear*. This image is seen throughout the film and is also the inspiration for the way Spielberg frames a shot early on as Jim's parents stand over his bed in their Shanghai home.

Like Elliot's, Jim's bedroom (both at home and in the

camp) is a cocoon of fantasy and dream and is clearly a vital survival source. When he pulls his ragged curtain across he is somehow safe, the wall covered with his favourite images from Life magazine.

Things are often not what they seem. When the nuclear explosion ignites in the sky the audience is aware of what it is but to Jim it carries a more benign meaning – again reinforcing Spielberg's ongoing affinity for some sense of an unseen, guiding presence, that angel on our shoulders.

Sound and Vision Keys: Flight as escape and also aspiration – Jim's wild shout as the B52s roar in, and his friendship with the kamikaze pilot. Resurrection – Jim tries to revive the kamikaze pilot after falling on his sword. 'I can bring them back I can bring them all back,' Jim breathlessly intones. The moment evokes *ET* and predates the conclusion of *Indiana Jones and the Last Crusade* and the bus driver sequence in *Always*. The death of Rufio in *Hook* is a fainter echo, as is the bloody death of Medic Wade in *Saving Private Ryan*. This motif of resurrection and the attempt to save the dying body makes physical the more spiritual aspect of Spielberg's stories, which, almost without exception, are narratives of rescue and revival. John Williams choir-heavy score accentuates the spiritual strain of the story. Spielberg's camera booms up to reveal a new world (the camp) rather like in *Close Encounters of the Third Kind* when Roy and Gillian discover Devil's Tower. *Empire of the Sun* is Spielberg's most surreal film, in keeping with Jim's faltering perception and judgement as it becomes increasingly warped and intense. For example, Jim's discovery of footprints in the powder on the floor of his parents' room and the moment when Jim thinks he has seen his mother in the doorway when in fact it is a Japanese soldier dressed in a robe. The Olympic stadium sequence is especially eerie and unsettling, whilst also being wondrous for its scale. There is a sense of a ruined world which Spielberg certainly returns to in *Saving Private Ryan*.

The moment of separation from family and ensuing desperation – when Jim loses his parents in the crowd in Shanghai and he leaps up onto the rickshaw and screams out for them.

One image directly echoes *The Sugarland Express* when Jim is about to cast his suitcase into the river and he stands in silhouette against sunlit golden water, a chapter of his life coming to an end.

Fantasy and play/imagination as necessary to survival – Jim discovers the crashed plane in the field at the party and dons sunglasses and sits in the cockpit pretending to fly. Yet too much insistence on play can catch you out – the very reason Jim is separated from his parents is because of his determination to go and pick up his toy plane amidst a huge crowd.

At the close of the film, Jim is reunited with his parents in a bombed-out conservatory but unusually and appropriately there is no rush of excitement or overwhelming sense of joy as in *The Color Purple*, *Close Encounters of the Third Kind* and *Indiana Jones and the Temple of Doom*.

Background: *Empire of the Sun* was Spielberg's second adaptation of a novel in a row and he began shooting after he was awarded the Irving Thalberg Award for Career

Achievement at the 1987 Oscars. Suffice to say, his work on the film is suitably inspired. Originally, David Lean was to have directed the film with Spielberg producing and Lean's influence on Spielberg is perhaps most evident in this film. *Empire of the Sun* was the first Hollywood film to be shot in Shanghai for many years. JG Ballard, the author of the novel, can be spotted early in the film in a John Bull outfit at the party. He also provides the voiceover at the start. *Empire of the Sun* was shot in London and southern Spain, where Spielberg returned a year later to shoot parts of *Indiana Jones and the Last Crusade*. Ben Stiller (*Meet the Parents, There's Something about Mary*) is one of the American POWs.

Verdict: A significant Spielberg film which marked the start (intended or not) of a new phase in his storytelling. 5/5

Schindler's List (1993)

Cast: Liam Neeson (Oskar Schindler), Ben Kingsley (Itzhak Stern), Ralph Fiennes (Amon Goeth), Caroline Goodall (Emilie Schindler), Jonathan Sagalle (Poldek Pfefferberg), Embeth Davidtz (Helen Hirsch), Malgoscha Gebel (Victoria Klonowska), Shmulik Levy (Wilek Chilowicz), Mark Ivanir (Marcel Goldberg), Beatrice Macola (Ingrid), Andrezj Seweryn (Julian Scherner), Freidrich von Thun (Rolf Czurda), Krysztof Luft (Herman Toffel), Harry Nehring (Leo John), Norbert Wiesser (Albert Hujar), Adi Nitzan (Mila Pfefferberg), Michael Schneider (Juda Dresner), Mirir Fabian (Chaja Dresner), Anna Mucha (Danka Dresner), Albert Misak (Mordecai Wulkan)

Crew: Director: Steven Spielberg, Producers: Branko Lustig, Gerlad R Molen, Lew Rywin, Steven Spielberg, Screenplay: Steven Zaillian, Cinematographer: Janusz Kaminski, Production Designer: Allan Starski, Editor: Michael Kahn, Music: John Williams, Special Visual Effects: Industrial Light and Magic, 197 minutes

Story: Poland. The Second World War. 1941. Nazi forces occupy Krakow and have divided the city into ghettos where Polish Jews are forced to live. Czech industrialist and Nazi party member, Oskar Schindler is in the process of establishing an enamelware factory and approaches Jewish investors to back it. Soon enough, Oskar has staffed the factory floor with Krakow Jews. It soon becomes apparent that those Jews in the factory are in effect safe from being taken to a death camp. Schindler has inadvertently created a haven. Initially uneasy with his growing reputation as a saviour figure, Schindler's commitment to the Jewish plight is transformed when he witnesses the liquidation of the ghetto. With the understated commitment of accountant Itzhak Stern (living in the ghetto and later at Plaszow Concentration Camp) Schindler schmoozes with the ruthless Amon Goeth and other high-ranking Nazi officials to ensure the protection of his Jews as essential labour towards the war effort. Schindler's political finesse results in him buying his Jews from Goeth's camp thereby ensuring their long-term safety in his factory in Plaszow, from where they are then transported to Schindler's hometown of Brinnlitz in Czechoslovakia. Terrifyingly, the train of women is routed to Auschwitz and only at the last minute is Schindler able to intervene.

Eventually, the war ends. The Jews are now free and Schindler becomes a war criminal. He says farewell to the people he has saved and disappears into the night. The film ends with present-day footage of the surviving Schindler Jews at the grave of Oskar Schindler.

Themes: Whilst on the surface being Spielberg's most atypical film to date (a perception the media played on fairly extensively) *Schindler's List* plays out Spielberg's fundamental dramatic concerns against a real world scenario that has not and must not be forgotten. *Schindler's List* serves as both an example of how complex the issue of recreating history through drama is and also stands as a piece of film craft in its own right regardless of its fidelity to a moment in time. Discussing the film during its release and also in retrospect, Spielberg rightly acknowledged its stylistic difference to virtually all his other films. In its drama, though, the film is one of his richest, most assured efforts and one which can be regarded as a watershed. From this moment on, it transformed his persona as a filmmaker and seemingly reinvigorated his storytelling sensibility in a way that segments of *Empire of the Sun* had hinted at six years before. There was a willingness to ease off on trademark devices in order to give the intensity of the drama and its context an immediacy. Of course one could argue, as Claude Lanzmann director of Holocaust documentary Shoah did, that the decision to film in black and white perhaps distances the audience from the reality the film refers to.

As in some of Spielberg's other movies, the drama is played out in an environment removed and immediately distinctive from everyday life. The concentration camp is an aberration, another world that allows the drama and its characters to exist in abstract, only to finally return them to the world that they left behind for a period of time. Oskar Schindler goes from a confident, assured character to, at the very end, an emotionally frail man, exhausted by his efforts. This closure for the film was deemed by some as sentimental and unnecessary at the time of the film's original release. It is, in fact, one of the key Spielberg moments in the film, adhering to the familiar themes of family, community and home. However, whereas usually the family and protagonist are reunited at the end of the film, in this piece the protagonist must say goodbye. And rather like Cinque handing the tooth to Joadson at the end of *Amistad* or *ET* leaving with his potted plant, Oskar is given a keepsake – a gold ring engraved with a Talmudic Law: He who saves one life, saves the world entire. Schindler leaves aware of how much he is loved, how much he belongs in the community he has become a part of. Schindler's journey has been transcendental – moving from material, pragmatic concerns to an immersion in a culture's tradition. Itzhak Stern throughout the film has a more ethereal presence – the id to Schindler's ego. Stern is cautious and wise – something of a Jiminy Cricket figure. Stern is the classic Spielberg character in this story, not Schindler. Stern's anxious, bespectacled features are not so far removed from those of Peter Banning, Matt Hooper, Roger Baldwin and Corporal Upham. History may judge Schindler a hero but in the drama of the film, Stern is the true saviour. Witness the scene where Stern finishes typing up Schindler's list. Spielberg charges the scene with a quasi-religious quality (partly thanks to John Williams' score) as Stern holds the papers up gently and protectively (rather like Commandments) and says: 'The list is an absolute good. The list is life.' The desk lamp is a key feature of the scene and so again we acknowledge Spielberg's visualisation of illumination. Indeed the very first image in the film is of a candle being lit in the darkness – a sense of the spiritual, the sacred.

Sound and Vision Keys: The film begins with an accumulation of names, testifying to the film's desire to register lives. Spielberg's extreme close-ups as names are typed out has an intensity to it accompanied by the hard, violent sound of the typing. This device recurs throughout the film. Spielberg employs a lot of hand-held camerawork.

For all of its crowd scenes the film never loses sight of the personal dramas being played out, such as the medical examination sequence and the horrifying liquidation of the ghetto in the middle of the film. It is perhaps this sequence which brought home the horror of the ethnic cleansing process. In this moment the film emphasises the destruction of tradition and the tiny details of desperate behaviour. The sequence is made the more horrific by Amon Goeth's voiceover as he prods his troops into action. Over shots of Jewish families anxious at their fate, we hear Goeth say: 'By this evening those six centuries [of Jewish life in Poland] are a rumour. Today is history.' Children are shown as being especially able to endure – most famously the little girl in red as she runs through the streets during the liquidation. For the first time Schindler's face is not confident and boyishly charming but instead distressed. This look of horror is amplified again later in the film when the bodies of Jewish people are exhumed and burned. This scene builds on some of the work of Empire of the Sun – a sense of everything that is normal being utterly eradicated. There is an overwhelmingly apocalyptic feeling to the sequence as the madness of the situation crystallises, notably when the wild-eyed soldier shoots repeatedly at the pyre of bodies. Over this scene the distraught sound of a choir carries over the images – it is piercing and uncomfortable to listen to. This scene of destruction is followed by a tearful, tender meeting between Oskar and Itzhak where they share a drink together, perhaps for the last time.

Spielberg elegantly wraps the personal dramas around recreations of history. In the film's stony grey poster the hand of an adult woman holds the hand of a child (the sleeve in the faintest hint of red). This promotional image emphasises the intimacy of the story – whilst Spielberg must acknowledge that a genocide occurred, his most usefully dramatic approach is to focus on individuals. The economy of style – the candle smoke match cutting to the trail of smoke from the train at the start of the film.

Stern is Schindler's conscience, his source of reason, something of a father figure, who is both frustrating and comforting. The film is like a buddy movie. Itzhak: 'Herr Director – don't let things fall apart, I work too hard.' Oskar: 'I'll look in on you – see how you are doing.' At the close of the film when the Jews and soldiers are gathered in the factory to hear Oskar address them, Oskar glances at Stern at one point and winks. It could be Indy winking to Short Round in *Temple Of Doom*. Oskar too exhibits protective fatherly qualities – Liam Neeson as a performer embodies a sense of bearish warmth, of protecting – a feature of his personality made evident from the outset. Schindler's List has a narrative based around rescue and the film carries a strong parallel with the story of Moses leading his people to freedom.

When Schindler refers to the Jews as his people, Goeth retorts with: 'My people? Who are you? Moses?' In 1998, DreamWorks SKG released the dazzling feature The Prince Of Egypt telling the story of Moses. Schindler's mission, his quest, is to ensure the safety of hundreds of Jewish people. He is a father figure in the largest sense possible, compelled to protect others in an extraordinary historical moment.

As such, whilst Schindler's real-world efforts have become the source of drama (based on the source novel Schindler's Ark by Thomas Kenneally) he becomes another in an ongoing line of Spielberg's heroes, though to date he may yet be his most complicated. Liam Neeson's facial resemblance to Harrison Ford only serves to enhance the character's place in the Spielberg canon.

Spielberg displays his skill as a director of actors by eliciting a nuanced performance from Ralph Fiennes as Amon Goeth, overlord of the death camp. Perhaps Goeth's most telling scene is when he talks to himself in the mirror revealing a very human frailty, which makes his violence more shocking. Schindler's List rightly advocates tolerance and testifies to a historic atrocity. By the close of the film, Schindler has been illuminated but may have learnt his lesson too late, breaking down as he realises he could have saved even more lives. Stern comforts Schindler who is then embraced by many – by his surrogate family.

Background: *Schindler's List* marked the start of a new collaboration for Spielberg with cinematographer Janusz Kaminski who had worked on an Amblin Entertainment television drama called *Class of 61* set in the US Civil War. Spielberg has worked with Kaminski since. It is one of his most productive collaborations, which has given Spielberg's images a refreshingly austere palette. Perhaps the word that most effectively defines Spielberg's aesthetic on *Schindler's List* is restraint.

Spielberg had bought the rights to the novel in 1982 but waited until he felt comfortable and confident to tell such a story in a certain way. At one point Martin Scorsese was to have directed with Spielberg producing. Spielberg made *Schindler's List* immediately after finishing filming on *Jurassic Park*. Whilst dinosaurs conquered digital imaging under the supervision of George Lucas, Spielberg was in Poland shooting *Schindler's List* overseeing Jurassic images via satellite on a daily basis.

Schindler's List received Oscars and numerous other awards and recognition and in a sense created a new directorial persona for Spielberg as 'recorder' of history. The film gave way to the Shoah Foundation and an expansive video archive documenting survivors' testimonies (www.shoahfoundation.org). The film, with its real-world environment, finally made clear what Spielberg had been saying all along in so many of his films: that community, love and tolerance are not to be forgotten.

Verdict: Spielberg reinvents his cinematic identity and proves cinema's power to illuminate and bring people together. The film showcases Spielberg's ability to be restrained in his storytelling and shows how strong a director of actors he is. 5/5

Amistad (1997)

Cast: Djimon Hounsou (Cinque), Morgan Freeman (Theodore Joadson), Nigel Hawthorne (Martin Van Buren), Anthony Hopkins (John Quincy Adams), Matthew McConaughey (Roger Baldwin), David Paymer (Secretary Forsyth), Pete Postlethwaite (Holabird), Stellan Skarsgard (Tappan), Razaaq Adoit (Yamba), Abu

Bakaar Fofanah (Fala), Anna Paquin (Queen Isabella), Tomas Milian (Calderon), Chjwetel Ejiofor (Ensign Covey), Geno Silva (Ruiz), John Ortiz (Montes), Ralph Brown (Lieutenant Gedney), Allan Rich (Judge Juttson), Paul Guilfoyle (Attorney), Peter Firth (Captain Fitzgerald), Arliss Howard (John C Calhoun), Willie Amakye (Folowa)

Crew: Director: Steven Spielberg, Producers: Debbie Allen, Robert M Cooper, Bonnie Curtis, Paul Deason, Laurie McDonald, Walter F Parkes (Executive Producer) Tim Shriver, Steven Spielberg, Colin Wilson, Screenplay: David Franzoni, Music: John Williams, Cinematographer: Janusz Kaminski, Editor: Michael Kahn, Visual Effects: Industrial Light and Magic, 152 minutes

Story: 1839. One of the African slaves from Sierra Leone, en route to America, breaks free of his chains and leads a frantic, violent escape from the Spanish boat the slaves are being held on. The slaves wash ashore on the eastern seaboard of America, are imprisoned and then brought to trial for their perceived crime. A debate develops around whether the slaves are property or people. A young idealistic attorney, Roger Baldwin allies with two abolitionists, Theodore Joadson and Lewis Tappan, to defend the rebel slaves, led by their charismatic leader Cinque. The case is initially won by the defence but is then taken to retrial. Ex-President John Quincy Adams is called upon to make the case for the slaves' freedom. The slaves are set free and return home.

Themes: Spielberg's first courtroom drama and his first directorial effort for his own studio, DreamWorks SKG. *Amistad* did not prove a popular draw with audiences despite its intelligent and mature recreation of a historical event and the issues of racism and intolerance. Spielberg shuffles deftly between the courtroom protocol, debates around freedom and property, and ensuring that his familiar concerns are given a platform. He also finds a space in the film to provide some context for the American Civil War. With *Amistad,* Spielberg confirmed his humanistic impulse which had really been apparent in all his work since *Duel.* The very title of the film, *Amistad,* means friendship and returns us to *Jaws'* town of Amity, which means the same thing. Baldwin must shift from practical, daily concerns to honouring a deeper, more eternal and meaningful issue, regardless of the consequences. The boyish, bespectacled Baldwin (dressed rather like Jiminy Cricket at the start of the film, and just as chipper in a way that Matt Hooper is in *Jaws*), embarks on a journey into the legal system and human rights whilst also developing a kinship with Cinque as they struggle to communicate. The three white men who aid Cinque are driven by a sense of mission first defined by Tappan: 'It is our destiny to save these people, they are people not live-stock.' As in *The Color Purple* and *ET*, sunlight pours in through windows with an almost supernatural power, as though some benign, unseen force is watching over the proceedings. Baldwin and Cinque forge a brotherhood which will ultimately be protected over by an older father figure in the form of John Quincy Adams. When first asked by Joadson and Tappan to aid them Adams rejects their invitation saying that they should, 'Find someone whose inspiration blossoms the more you lose.' A classic line for a Spielberg film. It would be just as appropriate in *Always*.

Where *Schindler's List*'s drama plays out amongst strong women, in *Amistad* and *Saving Private Ryan,* Spielberg chooses almost exclusively male worlds in which to tell his stories.

Amistad is another permutation on his rescue story motif as the abolitionists fight to free the African slaves. The young and idealistic Roger Baldwin, bespectacled in classic Spielberg tradition, allies himself with his own mentor figures in the abolitionists – just as Schindler did with Itzhak Stern.

The film, rather like *Close Encounters of the Third Kind*, is very much concerned with communication – witness Baldwin's frustration as he tries to explain having to retry the case to Cinque via an interpreter, Covey. The spoken word is insufficient. The *Close Encounters* connection is made stronger still when you consider how Cinque's character is initially defined as being something of a star-man. Following the slave and captors' battle Cinque calmly and quietly steers the boat across the sea. Spielberg's camera is placed at Cinque's feet looking up, the stars glistening above Cinque as he turns the boat. Cinque possesses the same gentility as ET and, as in that film, the outsider must ally with a 'local' to find a way to survive the chaos and uncertainty that ensue, all the while just wanting to get back home. When Cinque explains to Baldwin how far he has come, the moment recalls ET elevating the toys in Elliot's bedroom to simulate a star system.

The film suggests how alien the environment is to the Africans. Cinque freaks out in court – he focuses on people's hands, canes, shoes before standing up and proclaiming, 'Give us free.' The slaves are in a sense lost children who must be protected by a group of fathers, the ultimate embodiment being the ex-President of the United States.

Amistad is very much a film about community, as the heroes join together to form an ad hoc family which must hold strong for the duration of the challenge at hand. As with *ET*, *Hook*, *Empire of the Sun* and *Saving Private Ryan*, the compulsion to get back home, kept appropriately vague so that the audience can transfer to it their own meaning of home, allows Spielberg to play on a favourite idea: memory and roots. Cinque tells Quincy Adams that he will call on the spirits of his ancestors to help him through the trials. In one scene, Baldwin and Covey encourage Cinque to recall his story about killing a lion, thereby proving his greatness. In retelling the story, Cinque is calling on the invisible guidance and support of his own angels (on his shoulders), 'I will call into the past and beg them to come and help me. I will reach back and draw them into me.'

Spielberg announces the drama's illuminating qualities by having sunlight stream in through windows in vast blocks of light slicing through smoky courtrooms. When Cinque returns home he sails towards the sunset. *Like Saving Private Ryan*, Amistad is a film about very different and sometimes confused and lost men banding together to overcome a seemingly impossible task. Baldwin says to Cinque: 'I'm all you've got. You're all I've got.' At his most desperate for guidance Baldwin writes to ex-President Adams, 'Sir, we need you. If ever there was a time for a man to cast aside his daily trappings and array himself for battle that time has come.' This plea applies to the cause of many Spielberg heroes.

In John Quincy Adams, Spielberg and Hopkins fashion a character who is beatific, becoming something of an ET figure — a font of knowledge, compassion and wisdom. Like ET, Spielberg associates Adams with flowers and cultivation, growth and beauty. The motif of the flower is important in this film — Adams makes reference to blossoming early in the film when he picks a rose. Adams is also frequently seen in his conservatory which is where he first speaks with Cinque. Spielberg's camera even accentuates the moment when Adams pushes a potted plant into the sunlight on the carpet of his study. Spielberg not only has Adams and Cinque examine a delicate African violet but also includes a pure white flower in the shots of Cinque's face.

Sound and Vision Keys: Spielberg uses extreme close-ups. When you first see Cinque's eyes in the flashing lightning it recalls an image from Jurassic Park. We are in a world of chaos and we have the primal urge to survive. Knowledge and wisdom and an understanding of history are qualities embodied in Adams who is associated with the white statues on display in the Supreme Court – they represent the purity of his character. Adams is also framed early in the film with clear blue skies above – a kind of purity of vision which he represents all through the film, culminating in his speech at the Supreme Court where Spielberg frames him against a statue of his father. Quincy is a benign father figure in the way Henry Jones, John Hammond (despite his confused intentions) and Captain Tanner are. Adams is on the side of the rebels, just as Captain Tanner is in *The Sugarland Express* and as Keys is in *ET*.

The Spielberg motif of hands making contact – Cinque puts Baldwin's hands to his chest at the end of the film and it recalls Elliot saying goodbye to ET. As at the end of *Schindler's List*, the freed character gives their advocate (their guardian, their angel) a gift. *In Schindler's List* it is a ring, in *Amistad* it is a tooth.

Spielberg economically intercuts between the judge at church praying (for guidance we assume) and Yamba and Cinque looking at pictures of Christ's life in a copy of the Bible. Cinque and Yamba respond to the images, finding a kinship with the story they tell. When the slaves are walked through town to court Yamba glances up at the three masts of a ship at dock and the crucifix connection is apparent.

Spielberg contrasts the rusty, warm browns of Adams' study and Baldwin's impoverished office with the opulence of the Queen of Spain's apartment and the cold grey marble of Martin Van Buren's offices. John Williams' strong score invokes Aaron Copland's music. The American material contrasts with the powerful African inflections of the stunning choral theme *Dry Your Tears Afrika*.

Background: The film was shot in the winter of 1997, immediately after *The Lost World: Jurassic Park*, and is the first Spielberg film to be set before the twentieth-century. In an interview, Spielberg stressed how he did not want the film to have a twentieth century movie feel. Instead his intention was for the static compositions to be more like paintings. The film's visual design and lighting approach was heavily influenced by the paintings of Goya. The film marks another in the very effective Spielberg-Kaminski collaboration. It is an understated film with, for Spielberg, a fairly static camera which only moves to emphasise key moments, such as when Cinque stands and shouts out in court. It is a moment of what Spielberg called an 'epiphany.'

Verdict: This is an underrated movie which is quite dialogue-heavy for a Spielberg piece yet, after Empire of the Sun, perhaps his most David Lean-like. More openly emotional an historical piece than *Schindler's List*. Perhaps more melodramatic. 4/5

Saving Private Ryan (1998)

Cast: Tom Hanks (Captain John Miller), Tom Sizemore (Sergeant Mike Horvath), Edward J Burns (Private Robert Reiben), Matt Damon (Private James Ryan), Jeremy Davies (Corporal Timothy Upham), Vin Diesel (Private Adrian Caparzo), Adam Goldberg (Private Stanley Mellish), Barry Pepper (Private Daniel Jackson), Giovanni Ribisi (Medic Harlan Wade), Ted Danson (Captain Brian Hamill)

Crew: Director: Steven Spielberg, Producers: Ian Bryce, Bonnie Curtis, Mark Gordon, Gary Levinsohn, Allison Lyon Segan, Steven Spielberg, Screenplay: Robert Rodat, Cinematographer: Janusz Kaminski, Editor: Michael Kahn, Production Designer: Thomas E Sanders, Music: John Williams, Visual Effects: Industrial Light and Magic, 168 minutes

Story: 1945. Omaha Beach and the Allied Forces storm the beaches of Normandy. We follow the soldiers under the leadership of Captain John Miller (a schoolteacher by vocation) as they come under intense German fire. After achieving their goal and surviving, Miller and his men are given an unexpected mission – to rescue Private James Ryan, the only surviving brother from a family who has lost its other three sons. Miller accepts the rescue mission and leads his soldiers on a quest to find the young soldier. As they cross the French countryside the soldiers debate the morality of the mission, risking many lives for one, and eventually find Ryan. Miller has to convince Ryan to come away from his unit in order to be returned home to his mother. In the shattered village of Ramelle, Miller and his soldiers face another force of Nazi power as tanks and soldiers attack. Miller is killed and Ryan survives.

Themes: *Saving Private Ryan* has one of the simplest storylines Spielberg has ever worked with, as slim and direct as those for *Duel*, *Jaws* and *Indiana Jones and the Temple of Doom*. Whilst some may decry the film as boring with the exception of its bookending action sequences, in my opinion the very elemental nature of the plot allows Spielberg to build around it yet another presentation of his age old concerns and anxieties. In a sense a companion piece to *Amistad* (and *Empire of the Sun*), *Saving Private Ryan* is a hymn to brotherhood and community in the face of chaos and aggression. Like *Always* , the film suggests that its characters are watched over by some guiding hand. The key line in *Saving Private Ryan* comes at the very end when Miller, dying, looks into the eyes of young James Ryan and whispers, 'Angels on our shoulders.' Two American planes roar overhead.

As with all of Spielberg's 1990s films, *Saving Private Ryan* shows a man struggling to protect others and not to forget his memories of home. When Miller meets Ryan he orders him not to leave his side, as though talking to a young child. The whole unit is in effect Miller's sons and so it is no surprise that such emphasis is placed on his real job as a high-school teacher. Like Martin Brody in *Jaws* and David Mann in *Duel*, John Miller is uneasy with the role of masculine endeavour – he is a cerebral figure. The first image we get of Miller is not of his face, but of his hands shaking. This uneasiness culminates when he removes himself from the group and cries – it recalls Neary in the shower crying when events have become too much for him to comprehend. His mirror character is Corporal Upham, bespectacled and more obviously uneasy with macho heroics. When Upham is introduced, the physical comedy that is part of his introduction is very reminiscent of some of the more human-scaled sight gags in *1941*. Sergeant Horvath however, revels in the man-of-action role. Once again, the drama centres on men who are lost and just want to get home. Miller says that the more times he kills a soldier the further from home he feels. This is a film virtually devoid of women, except for in one of the best sequences Spielberg has ever directed: the military discovering the Ryan brothers' link and informing their mother on her farm. At the farm, the sequence evokes Spielberg's porch scenes in *The Color Purple*. It is an economical scene that omits the one expected element – a shot of Mrs Ryan's tearful face. Ten years previously Spielberg probably would have shown the face breaking into tears and a Saving Private Ryan production still shows that such a shot was clearly made but not included in the final edit. Mrs Ryan is not made that specific. She comes to represent every mother. We only see her in silhouette at the sink or from behind as she collapses on the porch. Spielberg has always enjoyed reflections and he brilliantly pulls focus from Mrs Ryan's eyes looking over the net curtain to the approaching car shown in the reflection. This sequence, this mini movie if you like, encapsulates the film's theme of family and loss. Spielberg also uses it to connect back to American history with its direct quote from Abraham Lincoln. *After The*

Color Purple, *Saving Private Ryan* may be Spielberg's most John Ford-inspired film.

As a quest and rescue narrative there is never any doubt that the heroes will achieve their goal. Instead the interest is in what happens along the way, which is essentially the compulsion in all of Spielberg's stories. The journey is what counts the most. Apart from the stunningly edited battles at each end of the film, *Saving Private Ryan* is a very quiet film and certainly very sombre. Like *Amistad* it is a more openly emotional historical drama than *Schindler's List*. Like that film though, Spielberg was criticised for the coda. In *Saving Private Ryan* we return to a veteran at the Omaha cemetery crying at a gravestone. It is a Spielberg moment. The man is saved because he has family who gather around him as he sobs helplessly, just as Schindler sobbed helplessly surrounded by his surrogate family. The connection between past and present is made.

The film also presents the issue of tolerance – when Upham is in a position to kill a German soldier he decides not to. There has been too much death already.

Sound and Vision Keys: Spielberg employs hand-held camera throughout much of the film, making action more immediate and lending it a vérité feel. The bombed-out village of Ramelle is suffused with the same spirit as *Empire of the Sun* – that sense of everything just sliding into the weird. For example, Edith Piaf playing on the gramophone as the soldiers await the Nazi attack.

As in *Jurassic Park* and *Jaws,* Spielberg suggests presence of great threat through sound and then through image. We hear the rumbling German tank long before we see it.

A very austere, simple film. We are at eye level much of the time. No swooping camera moves – the most graceful sequence is the Mrs Ryan episode. Again, Spielberg uses extreme close-ups on eyes as in *Amistad*.

In the church where the men camp Spielberg uses candlelight.

Saving Private Ryan is notable for its spare use of John Williams' score. None of the action scenes are scored, only by sound design and synchronous effects. Instead, the music score underscores the quiet, dialogue scenes so that it is not being used to intensify the experience of battle or symbolise it but instead speaks of loss, home and the desire to go home.

Background: Immediately after filming *Amistad* Spielberg shot *Saving Private Ryan* on location in Ireland and Hertfordshire. The original Robert Rodat screenplay was more of a comedy until Spielberg came on board and put it through several more drafts, including one by Frank Darabont, writer/director of *The Shawshank Redemption* and *The Green Mile*.

The World War II photographs of Robert Capa were very influential in the images and sequences of the Omaha Beach landing. The film colour was desaturated to make it feel like archive footage. The shutter speed on the camera was designed to give the images a sense of reality, lacking the blur that typically appears in any motion picture when something moves across the frame.

Verdict: Classic Spielberg; arguably a companion piece to *Empire of the Sun*. The sombre tone of this movie also anticipates the emotional shadows found in *AI* and *Minority Report*.5/5

Shadows, Doubt and Little Rays of Sunlight: *AI: Artificial Intelligence, Minority Report* and *Catch Me If You Can.*

AI: Artificial Intelligence

Time will be kinder to *AI: Artificial Intelligence* than the box office was and it will likely emerge as one of Spielberg's greatest films. The Stanley Kubrick association is worth acknowledging up to a point and the collaboration between the two directors over the movie's long gestation is intriguing. The resulting film, though, is far more Steven than Stanley.

Kubrick had pitched the idea for the film to Spielberg back in 1984 and Spielberg kept a vow of silence about it. *AI*'s roots are in a short story written by Brian Aldiss called *Supertoys Last All Summer Long.* The initial concept is expanded greatly by the film and Ian Watson's screen-story, from which Spielberg developed his screenplay, and Aldiss followed the original piece with two sequential shorts about his robot boy David which inform the larger narrative. Aldiss was not a big fan of Kubrick's ambition to integrate the Pinocchio motif into the film treatment of his short story.

AI's premise charts a robot boy's desperate quest to be loved and belong. Initially a gift from a husband to his wife, to compensate for their own absent son, the robot boy is eventually abandoned in the woods and must fend for himself. The boy is befriended by an adult robot, Gigolo Joe, who helps the boy David in his trek to find the Blue Fairy whom David believes will make him a real human. En route, Joe and David are threatened with 'death' at the hands of humans who are engaged in a kind of techno race hatred towards the robots of the world. Spielberg explained that the thinking was that orga (humans) and mecha (robots) were on the edge of civil war.

In 1993, Kubrick, impressed by the CGI effects of *Jurassic Park* started developing the film but found the technology frustrated him. At one point he considered an animatronic figure for David but Kubrick's work with Chris Cunningham (effects artist and pop promo director) did not solve the dilemma. Kubrick's other collaborator before Spielberg agreed to direct the film (in the wake of Kubrick's death in March 2000) was British comic book artist Chris Baker who generated countless concept designs and storyboards, all of which Spielberg had to complement Kubrick's ninety-page treatment. What is most potent in the film is its undiluted celebration of the mother figure (always a strong character in Spielberg's film) and the veneration is made absolute in the images of, and connections made, between the Virgin Mary, the Blue Fairy and Monica. The film is suffused with a sense of grace and spirituality that recalls *Close Encounters of the Third Kind (1977)* and *Always (1989)*.

With *AI* the sense was that Spielberg had been able to throw open the door to images and associations he had been storing up for many years, and the film that most readily came to mind was his 1987 movie Empire of the Sun, a film spiked with apocalyptic images. In contrast, Spielberg's love of musicals is manifest at points throughout *AI*, such as in the shot of Gigolo Joe dancing down the rainy street and along the kerb. Indeed, Spielberg had suggested to Jude Law (portraying Gigolo Joe) that part of his preparation for the role would be to watch Gene Kelly and Fred Astaire films. Jude Law as Gigolo Joe with his dancing in the moonlight, splashing through a pool of water, certainly suggests a futureworld Gene Kelly.

Like *Schindler's List*, *AI* makes a big moment out of a lost, threatened child holding hands with a protective adult in a world where racism has found a new identity – David clings to Gigolo Joe at the Flesh Fair, the brutal circus where humans (orga) watch robots (mecha) being torn to pieces or fired from canons for sport. Perhaps the easiest way to suggest the tonal difference between *AI* and *ET* is that in the latter film the full moon promises hope and joy. In *AI* the full moon (revealed as not quite that anyway) is a harbinger of doom. The film's forest sequence is perhaps its high point, suggesting vividly the film's fairy tale roots and revelling in them (as borne out by the visit to Dr Know) whilst also suggesting the artifice and emotional authenticity of a classic American narrative *The Wizard of Oz*. The film embraces eeriness with David's presence in the home and concludes with a sense of homecoming, love and also immense loss. Teddy is a Jiminy Cricket figure for David. Spielberg had suggested naming Teddy Mr Jingles but Kubrick insisted that it had to just be Teddy. For Teddy's voice, Spielberg's reference point was Eeyore in the Disney adaptation of the Winnie the Pooh stories.

For the overwhelming sense of a lost and broken world that the film conjures, there are moments where benevolence can be found and certainly the most unexpected but striking example of this is in the scene when David, dropping through the sea, is protected and guided by a shoal of fish.

AI is at its most engaging and exciting in the way it goes beyond its surface notion of whether or not a robot could behave in a human way and the degree to which a human can 'care' about a machine. The film's end sequences in which David dreams a return home sees him lit with very hot backlight that invests the moment with a sense of the divine and perfect. When he sits with the lead robot on his bed and has all things explained the two characters are framed by a circular bedroom window, creating a halo effect that recalls similar images in *ET: The Extra Terrestrial*. Hanging from the ceiling is a tiny mobile, of Peter Pan and Wendy.

AI was undoubtedly one of Spielberg's splashy, effects heavy dramas. As with *Jurassic Park*, Spielberg collaborated with Stan Winston in the creation of the mecha (robots) notably in the sequence set in the forest where David accidentally meets a 'family' of them. The mecha are mostly terrifying to look at, but in their robot hearts they are very human. Industrial Light and Magic, whose work on the film is truly beautiful, (Dennis Muren again collaborating) excelled in their creation of Rouge City, Dr Know, the

Blue Fairy (voiced by Meryl Streep) and most strikingly the far future world of an arctic earth, where Manhattan is submerged beneath ice. Some audiences were confused by the ending thinking the Giacometti-like characters that that discover David still alive beneath the ice were aliens when in fact they were the most refined robots yet, which in Spielberg's screenplay were dubbed Specialists. Hugely benevolent and graceful their faces were suggested by a warm spray of light and the indication of a smile, their angelic softness is critical to the film's dramatisation of spiritual ideas.

Some felt that *AI* would have been better had it finished with the image of the fallen Ferris Wheel (momentarily reminding us of *1941*) incarcerating David beneath the sea. Instead the film launches into a final dream state, the gentility and honest emotion of which is very affecting, although one could claim that some of the voice over by Ben Kingsley, whilst elegant and moving, has a clumsiness to it as Spielberg works to include everything in the film's summation.

For all the spectacle that weaves through the film its final image reminds audiences of its emphasis on what it means to have a home; the need for emotional security as we watch David lying next to his mother, Teddy watching over them, the moment framed by the window frame as Spielberg's camera gently draws us out of the story to return the audience to reality.

Of *AI*, Janusz Kaminski said: 'You could call this a modern *ET*. It's another instalment that deals with a very sophisticated world.' (JK, They Sing the Body Electric, Premiere, Fred Schruers, vol 14, no.10, June 2001, p. 52)

The film's powerful sense of reality slipping and shifting in a moment echoes the great facility Spielberg displayed with this flip-flopping of tone in Empire of the Sun. For Spielberg one of the appeals of the project was that 'it was a complicated piece of sci fi esoterica.' ('Report Card: The Steven Spielberg Interview' by Anthony C. Ferrante, p. 42, Cinescape, number 62, July 2002)

Despite its modest popular success several critics, notably Armond White (nobody writes with more enthusiasm about Spielberg than White) writing in The New York Press, recognised the film as a great pop movie, including it in his Ten Best Films ever list for the Sight and Sound poll of 2002. White's rhapsody for the film is fascinating. In his review he wrote that the film was 'as profoundly philosophical and contemplative as anything by cinema's most thoughtful, speculative artists – Borzage, Ozu, Demy, Tarkovsky . . . Moments that Kubrick would have made cold and ugly are surpassed by Spielberg's richer truth.' (From NY Press, volume 14, issue 26) AI is undeniably a celebration of the great, almost unfathomable love, between mothers and their sons which exceeds time and space.

Minority Report

Before AI had even been released, Spielberg was in the midst of directing the harsh futuristic thriller Minority Report, a film he had been talking about making since 1997, based on the short story by Philip K. Dick. Spielberg and Tom Cruise had been looking to make a film together since the 1980s. Famously they almost worked together on

Rain Man, which was eventually directed by Barry Levinson. In the early 1990s Cruise and Spielberg had considered making a film called *The Curious Case of Benjamin Button*, based on an F. Scott Fitzgerald story about a man who gets younger as the years pass.

Minority Report follows John Anderton, hotshot cop, whose personal life is in shreds since the death of his son and subsequent break up of his marriage. John finds himself framed for a murder he has yet to commit and with the help of a future seeing young woman (a precognitive), John sets out to prove his innocence.

Its warm coda aside, the film is the bleakest Spielberg has ever made and its nervousness and urban gloom is backed up by Janusz Kaminski's comment that 'Steven and I are fascinated by the look of the movies of the Seventies like *The French Connection*.' (AC, July 2002, vol 83, no.7, p. 35 Criminal Intent by Jay Holben)

In contrast to the lavish and soft visuals found in much of *AI*, the film has a severity unusual for a Spielberg picture. There is an austerity about it too that is as bare as Agatha's scalp. One of the movie's most arresting images is of John and Agatha caught in profile, their heads so close together, as he holds her, they almost become one. Indeed, if the film were to have ended with John Anderton's incarceration in a cemetery like prison it would have been unremittingly so.

The film has a darkness that hews very close to a Grimm's' fairy tale as its hero struggles to understand the shifting, dubious world around them. John's encounter with the eyeless man at night sets this fairy tale feeling in motion.

Other key scenes include the moment when John realises his son is missing, this is more terrifying than any hi tech terror (such as the spyders who recall the velociraptors of *Jurassic Park*) and brings to mind the crowd scenes on the beaches in Jaws. Just as AI used the woods vividly, so too Minority Report's heart lies in the sequence set in the garden and conservatory of an ageing scientist. The familiar Spielbergian sense of the mystical plays out in the character of Agatha, a lost girl as alien in many ways as ET and certainly as adrift. Both Agatha, and Spielberg's far from home alien, share a wide-eyed sense of enthrallment and terror gives way to great gentility and a wellspring of hope. When she envisions John's son playing on a beach she is framed and lit rather like the alien at the end of *Close Encounters* the image overexposed slightly. It also recalls the first time David is seen in *AI*.

Minority Report has its share of kinetic thrills. (Particularly notable is the rocketpack chase, which in such an era of digital effects was largely achieved with camera effects – a huge gantry system was constructed to allow multiple actors to fly on wires which were then erased in postproduction.) But its standout scenes are marked by black humour and centre far less on stunts and spectacle. The most potent moments are when John at home looking at a hologram of his dead son and the set piece in which John and Agatha escape the authorities through a shopping mall. John's adventure with Agatha reawakens his fatherly instincts as he must protect the near sacred Agatha from harm. One of the most stunning images sin the film is not anything obviously kinetic or splashy but rather a wonderful shot of John and Agatha, their heads in profile as he holds her. For that moment their emotional connection is powerfully visualised and their dependence on one another recalls the life support that ET and Elliot offer one another. Agatha is like a rag doll awakened to the world and ready to collapse at any moment.

Minority Report was shot largely in Washington DC, its futurescape expanded by ILM and the film marked Spielberg's most extensive use of visual effects since *Close Encounters of the Third Kind*, though not perhaps in the way expected. Much of its visual effects quota manifested itself in multilayered images on a viewscreen in Anderton's police base. The film did feature flying police ships and a digitally expanded cemetery for criminals that was chilling.

For all its bleakness Spielberg's affinity for the happier ending shines through which may suggest its fairy tale aspects over all else. Certainly, when John visits the aging woman scientist responsible for the Precog programme, his entrapment in the vines suggests a magic garden in which secrets will be revealed.

In the years prior to the production of *Minority Report*, claims were made that it was to be Spielberg's most cynical film, as though cynicism is perhaps better and cooler than sincerity and some strain of optimism. Sure enough on the eve of the film's release Spielberg said ' it went from being a cynical story to being a movie about wishful thinking.' (WIRED, p. 112).

There is a case to put that *Minority Report* is stronger in parts than as a whole. Cruise's performance is terrific and there are plenty of ideas and emotions at work but the density of its first half is not matched by its second in the overall scheme of things. It *is* stronger in part than whole but its overwhelming sense of anxiety recalls that of *Duel*, Spielberg's early TV movie, which like *Minority Report* was a chase. Indeed, where Spielberg had evoked the spirit of Hitchcock in *Jaws* he does so even more potently in *Minority Report* which is akin to *North by Northwest* and *Foreign Correspondent,* in fact, Spielberg references directly the scene in that movie where an assassin sidles off into a rain-drenched crowd, his escape aided by a forest of umbrellas. It is not unusual for a director to openly work in genres and ways that suggest their influences. *Saving Private Ryan* had its Howard Hawks quality, *Empire of the Sun* its David Lean inflections, *Hook* its Minnelli spirit and *The Color Purple* its John Ford soul.

Catch Me If You Can

Catch Me If You Can was announced as Spielberg's next movie in the late summer of 2001 and he filmed it in the winter and early spring of 2002. The film was based on the memoirs of real life fraudster Frank Abagnale. The project had been at DreamWorks for a while Cameron Crowe and Milos Forman had both been in the running to make it but eventually it came to Spielberg, who had been patiently monitoring its progress. *Catch Me If You Can* follows young Frank Abagnale as he realises his gifts as a conman whilst all the time being doggedly pursued by a benevolent FBI agent. The film was released in December 2002 and marked another collaboration with Tom Hanks and starred Leonardo Di Caprio as another Spielberg lost boy helped out by a surrogate father in Hanks's character. Like many Spielberg films, *Catch Me If You Can* is a road movie and its freewheeling, youthful energy is matched by a nicely judged sense of sadness. Spielberg commented that Frank 'was sent out into the world pretty much alone and was trying to find out who he was.' (Film Review, p. 29, Feb 2003, no. 627, Spielberg Plays Catch) John Williams' sax based score is delightful, notably his energetic theme for Frank and the low-key theme for the father. Both Frank and his father are lost boys. The film's small scale was a relief for audiences as well as for the filmmaker it seems and whilst his most playful film since *Always* was also one of his most fun and all out entertaining. The lightness of touch required by the story seems to have been a welcome alternative from Spielberg's darker outings – the last film that approached this sense of all out fun (regardless of whether it achieved it) was *Hook*. For inspiration Kaminski looked at Fred Wiseman's amazing documentary *High School* (Fred Wiseman, 1969) and of the overall visual design for *Catch Me If You Can*, Kaminski said 'I would compare the film's look to a bottle of champagne . . . the lighting style is very warm.' (AC, Karma Chameleon, Jan 2003 by John Pavlus, vol 84, no. 1, p. 64)

In all three of these films, the hero struggles to find their place in the world, and eventually secures it. *AI* is the major achievement, *Minority Report* and *Catch Me If You Can* offer more than enough interest but their emotional impact is not as immense as *AI*.

Musical Notes

Spielberg's collaboration with composer John Williams is legendary and these three most recent films offer Williams rich opportunities to write striking themes. *AI* is defined by its modernist approach to suggest the hard-edged future, Williams's composition suggesting the work of contemporary American composer John Adams. By contrast his material to describe the relationship between David and his mother Monica is ultra lullaby like and emphasises just how gentle the film is. Indeed, this gentleness has formed much of the appeal of all Spielberg's movies. For *Minority Report*, Williams wrote what Spielberg in his notes for the CD release calls a 'black and white' score which is a nod to Bernard Herrman's work on *Psycho* (Alfred Hitchcock, 1962). The highlight of Williams's score for Minority Report, though, is its soft and very sad piece reflecting the relationship between John and his lost son, Sean. Emphasising the piano, the piece recalls some Williams's work for the films *The Eiger Sanction* (Clint Eastwood, 1975) and *The Accidental Tourist* (Lawrence Kasdan, 1988). With *Catch Me If You Can*, the Spielberg-Williams collaboration took a new, fresh and thrilling turn, the orchestral score as energetic and joyful as excerpts from an Indiana Jones piece where needs be but also suffused with a jazzy energy indicating the period the film is set in. The score is one of the most surprising for the director and composer and also a highlight of their collaboration.

Future Pictures: *The Terminal* and Beyond

Throughout his career, Spielberg has developed ideas and projects that have, for one reason or another, not made it to the big, or small, screen. Originally, Spielberg had been due to direct *Big Fish*, based on the novel by Daniel Wallace, the film was eventually made by Tim Burton. Spielberg had hoped for Jack Nicholson to essay the role of Edward Bloom as an old man. From Spielberg's own comments about the development of the script, it appears that he became caught up in embellishing the story, introducing, perhaps, too many amendments and adding extraneous new scenes. In any event, the completed Burton movie was not outstanding, only flashes of director's flair shine through. Spielberg also passed on *Harry Potter and the Philosopher's Stone* but had stated that the third novel in the Harry Potter series, *Harry Potter and the Prisoner of Azkaban*, would have made an interesting challenge for him as a director.

In spring 2003 there was speculation that Spielberg might collaborate with Jim Carrey on a new movie version of James Thurber's short story *The Secret Life of Walter Mitty*, Mitty being something of an essential Spielberg manchild hero. As ever, news of a new Spielberg movie typically prompts interest and expectation but it remains to be seen if this project, like so many before it, gets beyond the development stage.

With *The Terminal* starring Tom Hanks due for release in June 2004, Spielberg continues working in the smaller movie format. It is intriguing to think how it will play out; *ET* is a very contained movie, for the most part, and its subsequent emotional impact was significant and enduring. In *Always* (1989) Spielberg had explored the love story format and *The Terminal* offers another sojourn into this terrain. Dramatising reality, the new movie involves a romance between Hanks's character, Viktor, and a stewardess named Amelia portrayed by Catherine Zeta Jones. In mid April 2004, the trailer for *The Terminal* was released and indicated a nicely relaxed visual style, somewhat akin to that of *Catch Me If You Can*. The trailer also suggested a tearjerker of a love story, peppered with comic touches. Within the garishly bright, an almost whiteout monotone that pervades the airport terminal, Spielberg and his cinematographer Janusz Kaminski find points at which to accentuate splashes of colour, such as in cluster of flowers on a table. The classic Spielbergian theme of loneliness and solitude comes ringing home (prompting us to connect images of the movie's hero with memories of ET reading quietly in a cupboard and of Frank in *Catch Me If You Can* imagining a new identity for himself to cope with his loneliness) material, much of it underscored by a cover version of John Denver's song *Leaving On A Jet Plane*. The film's tagline 'Life is waiting' is at once gently ironic and also indicative of the expected upbeat swing of the film.

The film continues the dazzling collaboration between Spielberg, Kahn, Kaminski and Williams. Certainly all of Spielberg's films have had their share of tender, quiet moments (think of the sweet scene between Frank and the nurse in the bedroom in *Catch Me If You Can* as a recent example).

So, as always in his career, Spielberg has continued to alternate between the fanciful and the more earthly with great skill and effect. His directorial work has continued to take audiences far away, yet there is always some sense of the familiar about his movies. With *The Terminal,* as with *The Sugarland Express* (1974), *Schindler's List* (1993) and *Amistad* (1997), a real person's situation is the heart and inspiration for the drama.

The Terminal centres on the life of a man whose national citizenship is rendered meaningless whilst he is at an airport because his home country undergoes a coup. The actual incident unfolded at Charles De Gaulle airport around a man named Merhan Karimi Nasseri (known as Sir Alfred) but *The Terminal* relocates the action to America and takes Nasseri's experience as its starting point. The film is not a factual representation of that man's life; in the movie, for example, the hero's nemesis is the Port Director. Certainly, the drama of a protagonist alone and away from home recalls *ET, Amistad* and the DreamWorks produced Tom Hanks movie *Cast Away* (Robert Zemeckis, 2000). Spielberg's interest in smaller scale stories is certainly fascinating and offers a welcome detour from the more expansive movies with which he has become synonymous. Having said that, the film again shows Speilberg's commitment to technical innovation and high production values; a disused hangar in LA was used to construct *the* airport terminal in. *The Terminal* has been written by Sacha Gervasi and redrafted by Jeff Nathanson who wrote the screenplay for *Catch Me If You Can*. The screenstory was written by Andrew Niccol, director of the accomplished science fiction movie

143

Gattaca (1997) and screenwriter of *The Truman Show* (Peter Weir, 1999). Niccol had originally been due to direct the film.

For all the potential small-scale drama of *The Terminal*, Spielberg's love of a good adventure story is due to see him return to the world of Indiana Jones someday soon. Talk of a fourth instalment in the series has been ongoing since 1997. In 2003, screenwriter Frank Darabont was commissioned to write the screenplay for the fourth film, generating much excitement amongst the film fan community. Spielberg had already indicated that the film might have something of the qualities of Richard Lester's *Robin and Marian* (1976) in its potential to explore the aging process in a character synonymous with all out adventure. Perhaps it would also recall Sam Peckinpah's movie *Ride the High Country* in which two aging cowboys undertake one last adventure.

At one point M.Night Shymalan, writer-director of *The Sixth Sense,* (1999) *Unbreakable* (2000) and *Signs* (2002), was to have undertaken the project but Frank Darabont's involvement was seen as a real gift to the new movie. Darabont's early screenwriting work had included scripts for George Lucas as a writer on the *Young Indiana Jones Chronicles* TV series. Darabont went on to write and direct the hugely popular *The Shawshank Redemption* (1994) and the mystical prison drama *The Green Mile* (1999). Darabont's love of the adventure genre, fused with his literary style and facility with character, made his involvement with the Indiana Jones project very promising. However, the anticipation for a fourth Indiana Jones movie for proposed release in summer 2005 was complicated when in early February 2004 Darabont's screenplay was perceived to need extensive revision by the producer George Lucas. At the time of writing, the fourth Indy movie, looks set to be delayed for a least a further year but Spielberg has confirmed that it will, ultimately, be made.

Spielberg's next two projects are of promising contrast. First there is a drama based on the Israeli intelligence service's efforts to find and bring to justice those who murdered the Israeli Olympic athletes killed at the 1972 Munich Olympics. In April 2004, Variety reported that Ben Kingsley had been cast in a major role. As a follow up to this project, Spielberg looks set to go back to the nineteenth century with a movie entitled *The Rivals* about two competing women opera singers.

Perhaps such a film would mark a return to the melodramatic pulse of *The Color Purple* and indeed satisfy Spielberg's self acknowledged love of the musical format. Indeed, on the DVD of *The Color Purple* Spielberg acknowledges that he has actually been making musicals throughout his career. There is currently a stage musical version of *Catch Me If You Can* in development and possibly one based on *The Color Purple*.

With Indiana Jones 4 on hold, might Spielberg yet return to the cinema of spectacle and fantasy? It appears to be so. In mid-March 2004, *Variety* announced that Spielberg was in development with Tom Cruise on a new version of the H.G. Wells novel, *The War of the Worlds*. David Koepp, screenwriter on Spielberg's *Jurassic Park* and *The Lost World*, is collaborating again on this project. Of course, *Deep Impact*, which Spielberg executive produced (he had considered directing it) in 1998 has some kinship with the Wells premise.

Whether the proposed movie, due to shoot in 2005, will be set in the past or present is yet to be made known. For many filmgoers for whom Spielberg is synonymous with spectacle the film has real potential and bears out Spielberg's industry savvy, as he continues to alternate between the quieter movies and the all-out crowd pleasers.

Alongside, his work for the cinema Spielberg's involvement with The Shoah Foundation (an archive of testimony established after the release of Schindler's List as a means of gathering together comment and information about the Holocaust and other instances of profound racial intolerance) continues and his studio DreamWorks SKG (established in 1994) continues to make hugely popular films such as *Shrek* (Andrew Adamson, 2001), *American Beauty* (Sam Mendes, 2000), *Cast Away* and *The Road to Perdition* (Sam Mendes, 2002), which was very much a Spielberg film, especially in its second half with its focus on a father and son.

As a major figure of American popular culture Spielberg's reach now extends to producing a mini series about one of the defining historical periods of America which in turn popular culture helped define: Spielberg is executive producing a mini series entitled *Into the West* is set in the Old West which is due to air in summer 2005. The series will follow two generations of pioneer families and two generations of native American families. Spielberg has always expressed a love of Westerns and yet frustratingly has never directed one (despite the longstanding rumours surrounding *Into the Setting Son*, the cowboy picture he was mooted to be working with Scorsese on). His Indiana Jones movies contain images derived from Western iconography and Spielberg's affinity for terrain and open spaces would easily find a home in the Western genre. *Indiana Jones and the Last Crusade* opens with something approaching a Western as it charts the first adventure of Indiana Jones's life. Indeed, an early draft of *Last Crusade* had begun with a shootout in a cantina.

Since the late 1970s Spielberg has executive produced a vast number of feature films and the next few years continue the tradition. Spielberg is executive producing *Memoirs of a Geisha*, which he had planned to direct in the late 1990s and had developed quite extensively from Arthur Golden's novel of the same name. Had Spielberg directed it might have interestingly supplemented *Empire of the Sun* in many ways. The movie now looks set to be directed by Rob Marshall who directed *Chicago* (2002).

Then too, there is a proposed feature version of Herge's Tintin. Spielberg had pursued a Tintin movie back in the mid 1980s. In early 2004, the suggestion was the production was moving ever closer to being realised with Spielberg producing. The Tintin adventure *Red Rackham's Treasure* was to be fused with several other Tintin stories to create an appropriately expansive adventure. *Zorro 2* is also in the works and DreamWorks Animation, which won the first Oscar for Animated Feature with *Shrek*, has *Madagascar*, *Shark Tale*, and *Over the Hedge* in production but has sadly closed down its classical animation division in the wake of the commercial failure of its feature *Sinbad* (2003).

Finally, there is the long gestating production *The*

Talisman, based on the vast novel by Stephen King and Peter Straub in which a boy named Jack Sawyer must venture into The Territories, an alternative modern America, in order to save his mother. The boy is aided by a walking, talking werewolf and as the novel's quotation from *Huckleberry Finn* suggests the spirit of Mark Twain plays its part in the fantasy. Indeed, Spielberg's affinity for Twain is not a surprise as the influence made itself known in *The Goonies* (there might be a sequel to that with the kids as grown ups) but also in his great sympathy for portraying young people on odysseys. Spielberg, who once considered directing *The Talisman* back in the 1980s, will now executive produce with new director Vadim Perelman, of *The House of Sand and Fog* (2003), directing.

In 2001, Spielberg said: 'I'm just a little more realistic about the world. That doesn't preclude me from making a movie some day of *Huckleberry Finn*, because I have that in me too.' (Resurrection Man, interview with SS by Jenny Cooney Carillo, Total Film, pp. 72-76, issue 57, October 2001, p. 76) Without getting too wrapped up in the Mark Twain affinity, *Minority Report* includes a reference to *Tom Sawyer*, Twain's classic novel of childhood.

For all of his more recent, apparently darker work, Spielberg has perhaps come full circle and now finds himself returning to the more obviously joyful aspects of his earlier films, which isn't to say that the more anxious heart doesn't continue to beat beneath the slick surface of his entertainments. Spielberg's sense of joy in film endures. The movies he directs continue to remind audiences of their shared pursuit for a place called home, wherever and whatever it might be.

Reference Materials
Bibliography

Steven Spielberg

Steven Spielberg, John Baxter, HarperCollins, 1996, ISBN 0002555875

The Films Of Steven Spielberg, Douglas Brode, Citadel Press, 1995, ISBN 0806515406

George Lucas: The Creative Impulse, Revised and Updated Edition, Charles Champlin, Virgin Books, 1997, ISBN 1852277211

The Future of The Movies: Interviews With Martin Scorsese, Steven Spielberg and George Lucas, Roger Ebert and Gene Siskel, Andrews and McMeel, 1991, ISBN 0836262166

Interviews: Steven Spielberg, edited by Lester D Friedman and Brent Notbohm, University Press of Mississippi, 2000, ISBN 157806113X

Postmodern Auteurs: Coppola, Lucas, De Palma, Spielberg And Scorsese, Kenneth von Gunden, McFarland and Company, Inc., 1991, ISBN 0899506186

Harrison Ford: Imperfect Hero, Garry Jenkins, Orion Books, 1997, ISBN 0684816946

Directors: Close Up, edited by Jeremy Kagan, Focal Press, 2000, ISBN 0240804066

Interviews: George Lucas, edited by Sally Keane, University of Mississippi Press, 1999, ISBN 1578061253

Steven Spielberg, Cheryl McAllister Saunders and Donald Mott, Columbus Filmmaker Series, 1986, ISBN 0862872735

Steven Spielberg, Joseph McBride, Faber and Faber, 1997, ISBN 0571191770

Industrial Light And Magic: The Art of Special Effects, Thomas G Smith, 1988, Columbus Books, ISBN 0862871425

Steven Spielberg, Philip M Taylor, Batsford Books, 1992, ISBN 0713466936

Biographical Dictionary of Film, David Thomson, Andre Deutsch Ltd, 1994, ISBN 023398599

Industrial Light and Magic: Into the Digital Realm, Mark Cotta Vaz and Patricia Rose Duignan, Virgin Books, 1996, ISBN 1852276061

Spielberg Films

Close Encounters of the Third Kind Diary, Bob Balaban, A Paradise Press Book Diary, 1978, ISBN 0931550009 – out of print

The Making of The Lost World: Jurassic Park, Jody Duncan, Boxtree, 1997, ISBN 0752224360

Spielberg's Holocaust, edited by Yosefa Loshitzky, Indiana University Press, 1997, ISBN 0253210984

Witness: The Making of Schindler's List, Franciszek Palowski, Orion Books, 1998, ISBN 0752817906

The Making of Jurassic Park, Don Shay and Jody Duncan, Boxtree, 1993, ISBN 1852837748

Behind the Scenes at ER, Janine Pourroy, Ebury Press, 1995,

ISBN 009181359X

Amistad: A Celebration of the Film, Steven Spielberg, essays by Steven Spielberg, Maya Angelou and Debbie Allen, Newmarket Press, 1997, ISBN 1557043515

Saving Private Ryan: The Men, The Mission, The Movie, Steven Spielberg and David James, Newmarket Press, 1998, ISBN 155704371X

The Same River Twice: Honouring the Difficult – A Meditation on Life, Spirit, Art, and the Making of the Film The Color Purple Ten Years Later, Alice Walker, The Women's Press Ltd, 1996, ISBN 0704344904

ET: The Extra Terrestrial: From Concept to Classic: The Illustrated Story of the Film and the Filmmakers, Pocket Books, 2002

The Films of Steven Spielberg: Critical Essays, edited by Charles L.P. Silet, The Scarecrow Press, Lanham, Maryland and Oxford, 2002

Articles

Suzanna Andrews, *The Man Who Would Be Walt*, interview with Spielberg in The New York Times (Arts and Leisure section), January 26 1992

David Breskin, *Steven Spielberg – From ET to TV*, interview in Rolling Stone 459, October 24 1985

Cinefex magazine, issues 18, 40, 44, 49, 53, 55, 65, 70, 75

Cinefex: issue 87 (*AI: Artificial Intelligence 'Mecha Odyssey'* by Joe Fordham) and issue 91 (*Minority Report 'Future Reality'* by Joe Fordham)

Richard Dyer, *Sounds of Spielberg*, Boston Globe, February 24 1998, discusses the recording of the score for *Saving*

Private Ryan and centres on an interview with Spielberg and John Williams

Simon Hattenstone, *Who's Afraid of Steven Spielberg? He is . . .* , The Guardian, September 11 1998

Henry Sheehan, *The Panning of Steven Spielberg: Chapter One of a Critical Cliffhanger*, Spielberg II, two articles from Film Comment, May–June 1992 (pp. 54–60), July–August 1992 (pp. 66–71)

Henry Sheehan, *The Fears of Children*, Sight and Sound, July 1993, (p.10)

The Amazing Stories Interview, Starlog 102, January 1986 (pp. 13–23)

Armond White, *Keeping up with the Joneses*, Film Comment, essay about *Indiana Jones and the Last Crusade*, summer 1989

Peter Wollen, *Theme Parks and Variations*, Sight and Sound, July 1993, (pp. 7–9)

American Cinematographer, July 1984 (*Indiana Jones and the Temple Of Doom*), August 1998 (*Saving Private Ryan*)

Miscellaneous

Lucasfilm Fan Club magazine, official publication that ran from 1987 until 1993 covering Lucasfilm projects, including *Indiana Jones and the Last Crusade* and *The Land Before Time*

Empire, British monthly film magazine has covered each Spielberg film since 1989 at the time of its release in Britain

Premiere Magazine, monthly American-published film

magazine (established in 1987), covered all of Spielberg's films as a director since *Indiana Jones and the Last Crusade*: June 1989, December 1989, December 1991, June 1993, January 1994, May 1997, January 1998, June 1998

Time Magazine, Spielberg has been the subject of several major interviews throughout his career in this worldwide publication. The following issues provide major interviews with him: May 31 1982 (*ET: The Extra Terrestrial*), July 15 1985 (Amblin Entertainment, *Amazing Stories*, *The Color Purple*), May 29 1989 (*Indiana Jones and the Last Crusade*), December 13 1993 (*Schindler's List*), March 27 1995 (Setting up DreamWorks SKG), June 16 1997 (*The Lost World, Amistad, Saving Private Ryan*, the future)

Close Encounters of the Third Kind, Collector's Edition magazine, 1977

The Goonies, Collector's Edition magazine, 1985

Back to the Future, Collector's Edition magazine, 1985

Raiders of the Lost Ark, Collector's Edition magazine, 1981

Indiana Jones and the Temple Of Doom, Collector's Edition magazine, 1984

Indiana Jones and the Last Crusade, Collector's Edition magazine, 1989

TV Interviews

Spielberg has given many TV interviews. The four below were particularly germane for this book:

Film 90, interviewed by Barry Norman, BBC1 March 1990

Face to Face, interviewed by Jeremy Isaacs, BBC2 March 1994

Film 98, interviewed by Barry Norman, BBC1 February 1998

Scene by Scene, interviewed by Mark Cousins, BBC2 September 1998

Filmography

2004: *The Terminal*

2002: *ET: The Extra Terrestrial* (20th Anniversary re-release), *Minority Report, Catch Me If You Can*

2001: *AI: Artificial Intelligence*

1999: *The Unfinished Journey*: short film for Millennium Celebrations

1998: *Saving Private Ryan*

1997: *Amistad, The Lost World: Jurassic Park*

1993: *Schindler's List, Jurassic Park*

1991: *Hook*

1989: *Always, Indiana Jones and the Last Crusade*

1987: *Empire of the Sun*

1985: *The Color Purple, Amazing Stories* episodes *Ghost Train* and *The Mission*

1984: *Indiana Jones and the Temple Of Doom*

1983: *Twilight Zone: The Movie* (*Kick the Can* story)

1982: *ET: The Extra Terrestrial*

1981: *Raiders of the Lost Ark*

1980: *Close Encounters of the Third Kind: The Special Edition*

1979: *1941*

1977: *Close Encounters of the Third Kind*

1975: *Jaws*

1974: *The Sugarland Express*
1973: *Savage*
1972: *Something Evil*
1971: *Duel, Owen Marshall: Counsellor at Law*: episode *Eulogy for a Wide Receiver, Columbo: Murder by the Book, The Psychiatrist* episodes *The Private World of Martin Dalton* and *Par for the Course*
1970: *Night Gallery* episode *Make Me Laugh, Marcus Welby, M.D* episode *The Gesture*
1969: *Night Gallery* episode *Eyes*
1968: *Amblin'*

Videos & DVDs

Duel VHS 0445263 (VHS release)
The Sugarland Express – unavailable
Jaws VHS 0539583 (VHS video) DVD UDR 90094 (DVD release)
Close Encounters of the Third Kind CVR 86501 (VHS release)
1941 VHS 0443043 (VHS release)
Raiders of the Lost Ark VHR 4392 (VHS release)
ET: The Extra Terrestrial VHR 6104 (VHS release)
Twilight Zone: The Movie – unavailable
Indiana Jones and the Temple of Doom VHR 4393 (VHS release)
The Color Purple DVD DO11534 (DVD release)
Empire of the Sun VHS SO11753 (VHS release)
Indiana Jones and the Last Crusade VHR 4394 (VHS release)
Always VHS 0618713 (VHS release)

Hook VHS CC7299 DVD CDR13187 (DVD release)

Jurassic Park VHS 0446523 DVD UDR90095 (DVD release)

Schindler's List VHS 0613473 (VHS release)

The Lost World: Jurassic Park DVD UDR90096 (DVD release)

Amistad VHS4900293 DVD 4909812 (DVD release)

Saving Private Ryan VHR4914 DVD PHE8040 (DVD release)

The Indiana Jones Trilogy DVD – all three features plus a series of featurettes focusing on special effects, sound, music and stunt work. The trailers for the films are also included.

Minority Report: this two-disc set features numerous short documentaries about the concept and production of the movie.

Catch Me If You Can: interviews with Spielberg, Hanks, DiCaprio, Abagnale *et al* alongside footage on location

Schindler's List

Band of Brothers box set

Taken DVD box set

Websites

www.dreamworks.com – official Website

www.shoahfoundation.com – Website for the Foundation established by Spielberg after Schindler's List

www.spielberg-dreamworks.com – comprehensive fansite, updated daily

www.starbright.com – Website for the charity that Spielberg is involved in to benefit children www.indianajones.com – official Website for the films

www.aimovie.com – Warner Brothers' official Website for the film

http://www.spielbergfilms.com – this is an incredibly comprehensive fansite covering Spielberg's efforts as both director and producer.

1903047773	Agatha Christie Mark Campbell	3.99
1903047706	Alan Moore Lance Parkin	3.99
1903047528	Alchemy & Alchemists Sean Martin	3.99
1903047005	Alfred Hitchcock NE Paul Duncan	4.99
1903047722	American Civil War Phil Davies	3.99
1903047730	American Indian Wars Howard Hughes	3.99
1903047463	Animation Mark Whitehead	4.99
1903047757	Ancient Greece Mike Paine	3.99
1903047714	Ang Lee Ellen Cheshire	3.99
1903047676	Audrey Hepburn Ellen Cheshire	3.99
190304779X	The Beastie Boys Richard Luck	3.99
1904048196	The Beatles Paul Charles	3.99
1903047854	The Beat Generation Jamie Russell	3.99
1903047366	Billy Wilder Glenn Hopp	3.99
1903047919	Bisexuality Angie Bowie	3.99
1903047749	Black Death Sean Martin	3.99
1903047587	Blaxploitation Films Mikel J Koven	3.99
1904048307	Bohemian London Travis Elborough	9.99hb (Oct 2004)
1903047455	Bollywood Ashok Banker	3.99
1903047129	Brian de Palma John Ashbrook	3.99
1903047579	Bruce Lee Simon B Kenny	3.99
1904048331	The Cathars Sean Martin	
190404803X	Carry On Films Mark Campbell	3.99
1904048048	Classic Radio Comedy Nat Coward	3.99
1903047811	Clint Eastwood Michael Carlson	3.99
1903047307	Conspiracy Theories Robin Ramsay	3.99
1904048099	Creative Writing Neil Nixon	3.99
1903047536	The Crusades Mike Paine	3.99
1903047285	Cyberpunk Andrew M Butler	3.99
1903047269	David Cronenberg John Costello	3.99
1903047064	David Lynch Le Blanc/Odell	3.99
1903047196	Doctor Who Mark Campbell	3.99
1904048277	Do Your Own PR Richard Milton	3.99
190304751X	Feminism Susan Osborne	3.99
1903047633	Film Music Paul Tonks	3.99
1903047080	Film Noir Paul Duncan	3.99
1904048080	Film Studies Andrew M Butler	3.99

190304748X	Filming on a Microbudget NE Paul Hardy 4.99 (July 2004)
190304765X	French New Wave Chris Wiegand 3.99
1903047544	Freud & Psychoanalysis Nick Rennison 3.99
1904048218	Georges Simenon David Carter 3.99
1903047943	George Lucas James Clarke 3.99
1904048013	German Expressionist Films Paul Cooke 3.99
1904048161	Globalisation Steven P McGiffen 3.99
1904048145	Hal Hartley Jason Wood 3.99
1904048110	Hammer Films John McCarty 3.99
1903047994	History of Witchcraft Lois Martin 3.99
1903047404	Hitchhiker's Guide M J Simpson 3.99
1903047072	Hong Kong's Heroic Bloodshed Martin Fitzgerald 3.99
1903047382	Horror Films Le Blanc/Odell 3.99
1903047692	Jack the Ripper Whitehead/Rivett 3.99
1903047102	Jackie Chan Le Blanc/Odell 3.99
1903047951	James Cameron Brian J Robb 3.99
1903047242	Jane Campion Ellen Cheshire 3.99
1904048188	Jethro Tull Raymond Benson 3.99
1904048331	Joel & Ethan Coen Cheshire/Ashbrook NE 4.99 (Nov 04)
1903047374	John Carpenter Le Blanc/Odell 3.99
1904048285	The Knights Templar Sean Martin 9.99 HB
1903047250	Krzystzof Kieslowski Monika Maurer 3.99
1903047609	Laurel & Hardy Brian J Robb 3.99
1903047803	The Madchester Scene Richard Luck 3.99
1903047315	Marilyn Monroe Paul Donnelley 3.99
1903047668	Martin Scorsese Paul Duncan 4.99 (Jul 2004)
1903047595	The Marx Brothers Mark Bego 3.99
1903047846	Michael Mann Mark Steensland 3.99
1903047641	Mike Hodges Mark Adams 3.99
1903047498	Nietzsche Travis Elborough 3.99
1903047110	Noir Fiction Paul Duncan 3.99
1904048226	Nuclear Paranoia C Newkey-Burden 3.99
1903047927	Oliver Stone Michael Carlson 3.99
1903047048	Orson Welles Martin Fitzgerald 3.99
1903047293	Philip K Dick Andrew M Butler 3.99
1904048242	Postmodernism Andrew M Butler 3.99
1903047560	Ridley Scott Brian Robb 3.99

1903047838	The Rise of New Labour Robin Ramsay	3.99
1904048102	Roger Corman Mark Whitehead	3.99
1903047897	Roman Polanski Daniel Bird	3.99
1903047447	Science Fiction Films John Costello	4.99 (Oct 04)
1903047412	Sergio Leone Michael Carlson	3.99
1903047684	Sherlock Holmes Mark Campbell	3.99
1903047277	Slasher Movies Mark Whitehead	3.99
1904048072	Spike Lee Darren Arnold	3.99
1903047013	Stanley Kubrick Paul Duncan	3.99
190304782X	Steven Soderbergh Jason Wood	3.99
1903047439	Steven Spielberg James Clarke	4.99
1903047331	Stock Market Essentials Victor Cuadra	3.99
1904048064	Succeed in Music Business Paul Charles	3.99
1903047765	Successful Sports Agent Mel Stein	3.99
1904048366	Tarantino D K Holm	4.99 (Nov 2004)
1903047145	Terry Gilliam John Ashbrook	3.99
1903047390	Terry Pratchett Andrew M Butler	3.99
1903047625	Tim Burton Le Blanc/Odell	3.99
190404817X	Tintin J M & R Lofficier	3.99
1903047889	UFOs Neil Nixon	3.99
1904048250	The Universe Richard Osborne	9.99 (HB)
190304717X	Vampire Films Le Blanc/Odell	3.99
190404820X	Videogaming Flatley & French	3.99
1903047935	Vietnam War Movies Jamie Russell	3.99
1904048129	Who Shot JFK? Robin Ramsay	3.99
1904048056	William Shakespeare Ian Nichols	3.99
1903047056	Woody Allen Martin Fitzgerald	3.99
1903047471	Writing a Screenplay John Costello	4.99

Available from all good bookshops or send a cheque to:
Pocket Essentials P.O. Box 394, Harpenden, Herts, AL5 1XJ.
Please make cheques payable to **'Oldcastle Books'**, add 50p for
postage and packing for each book in the UK and £1 elsewhere.

Customers worldwide can order online at
www.pocketessentials.com